CCNY MADE

MADE

Profiles in Grit

RONNYJANE GOLDSMITH

THE
History
PRESS

Published by The History Press
Charleston, SC
www.historypress.com

First published 2023

Manufactured in the United States

ISBN 9781467155175

Library of Congress Control Number: 2023938409

CONTENTS

ACKNOWLEDGEMENTS

This book could not have been completed without the tireless work and dedication of Vanessa Ioannidi.

I had the good fortune to be introduced to Vanessa by Dr. Miles Orvell, professor of English at Temple University. At that time, Vanessa was completing her master's degree, and I was looking for a student to assist me in completing *Temple Made: Profiles in Grit*. The timing could not have been better. Vanessa introduced me to the art of outlining and the skills required to develop social media content. I like to think that the experience working with a team to bring *Temple Made* to publication provided Vanessa with invaluable experience that added luster to her résumé and caught the eye of her current employer.

Vanessa received her BA (2019), summa cum laude, and MA (2020) in English language and literature from Temple University. While at Temple, she participated in the London Internship Program of the College of Global Studies at Arcadia University. After receiving her MA, she completed the Columbia University Graduate School of Journalism Publishing Course.

Subsequent to completing her graduate degree and bringing *Temple Made* to publication, Vanessa was hired by Simon & Schuster in New York City as a sales coordinator and liaison between production, managing editorial, design and accounts. The timing (and the location) of this position was perfect. It resulted in a two-year collaboration between Vanessa and me and the publication of *CCNY Made: Profiles in Grit*.

I would be remiss not to also acknowledge the support and encouragement of Vincent Boudreau, president, The City College of New York; Dee Dee Mozeleski, vice-president of the Office of Institutional Advancement, Communications and External Relations; and Banks Smither, acquisitions editor at Arcadia Publishing/The History Press.

Several years ago, over lunch in San Francisco, I approached Vince and Dee Dee with the idea for this book. Although I am not a CCNY alumni, and despite intentional and unintentional delays, they never doubted my commitment to writing *CCNY Made: Profiles in Grit*.

Banks Smither took a chance on a new book concept that brought *Temple Made* and *CCNY Made* to publication. Five years ago, I called Arcadia Publishing to order a dozen copies of a book about the history of The City College of New York. A conversation with the sales department led to a suggestion that I speak with Banks about writing a book about Temple University. While I was not interested in writing about the history of Temple, I suggested a different perspective, a book about alumni who started with very little and rose to the pinnacle of their professions. Banks was interested, and *Temple Made* was born. A second book followed, and like the first, the rest is history—or, more specifically, *CCNY Made*.

BEHIND THE BOOK

Note on Sources and Content

The profiles in *CCNY Made: Profiles in Grit* were not authorized by the subjects, none of whom was interviewed, nor did they review their profiles before publication. All information was obtained from public sources, including oral histories documented in the bibliography section of this book.

Due to the limitations of time, space and available information, thirty-two alumni—including four fictional alumni—were chosen to be profiled in this book.

It would be negligent if I did not acknowledge all those CCNY alumni living and deceased not included who, like those included, overcame poverty, adversity and setbacks to achieve greatness. Their perseverance and accomplishments are not forgotten.

Proceeds from *CCNY Made: Profiles in Grit*

In 2018, Ronnyjane Goldsmith established the Delancey Street Fund at CCNY. The fund is named after the street of the same name in New York City that gave immigrants to America a chance for a better life. The Delancey Street Fund provides assistance to students without financial resources who are facing catastrophic life events. All proceeds from the sale of *CCNY Made: Profiles in Grit* are dedicated to the Delancey Street Fund.

INTRODUCTION

You may not recognize their names, but you will recognize their accomplishments.

- They were champions of the common man and the underdog.
- They faced controversy and rejection before success.
- They were self-avowed or unjustly accused socialists and communists.
- They were responsible for discovering the vaccine that eradicated polio from the world.
- They wrote books and screenplays like *The Jungle*, *The Godfather* and *What Makes Sammy Run?*
- They were awarded Academy Awards, Tony Awards and the Pulitzer Prize.
- They were responsible for the historic brief in *Brown v. Board of Education*, the Supreme Court case that led to the desegregation of public schools; the creation of the International Criminal Court headquartered in The Hague; and the passage of the Meat Inspection and the Pure Food and Drug Acts.
- They continue to entertain us though their music like *Porgy and Bess* and "Somewhere Over the Rainbow."

- They include a U.S. Supreme Court justice, a chairman of the Joint Chiefs of Staff, three New York City mayors and the CEO and chairman of the board at Intel.

- Their portraits grace eighteen U.S. postage stamps and thirteen magazine covers.

And they all have one thing in common: they are CCNY Made.

What Is CCNY Made?

"Open the doors to all....Let the children of the rich and the poor take their seats together and know of no distinction save that of industry, good conduct, and intellect." These are the words of Townsend Harris and the essence of CCNY Made.

Founded as the Free Academy of the City of New York in 1847 by Harris, CCNY was originally a combination of a secondary school and college created to provide children of immigrants and the poor access to free higher education based on academic merit alone.

This book profiles thirty-two alumni, including four fictional alumni, who are CCNY Made.

Who Should Read *CCNY Made: Profiles in Grit*?

This book should be read by:

- Every person considering attending CCNY.

- Every student currently enrolled at CCNY.

- Every CCNY alumni.

- Anyone interested in the story of people who persevered and overcame poverty, adversity and setbacks to achieve greatness and improve the lives of their generation and the generations that followed.

Chapter 1
ART AND DESIGN

THE PHOTOGRAPHERS

Alfred Stieglitz, William Klein and Garry Winogrand are all ranked on *Professional Photographer* magazine's list of the 100 most influential photographers of all times—Stieglitz at no. 72, Klein at no. 25 and Winogrand at no. 17.

Although their lives spanned more than one hundred years and three centuries, Stieglitz, Klein and Winogrand have the distinction of each being considered a father of street photography, the genre of photography that records everyday life in a public place, often without the knowledge of the subject.

By introducing new techniques into the medium of photography, Stieglitz, Klein and Winogrand each in his unique way transformed photography into an undisputed fine art form for the twenty-first century.

Alfred Stieglitz

CCNY
ATTENDED 1880

Alfred Stieglitz was born in 1864 in Hoboken, New Jersey. Unlike many of the CCCNY alumni profiled in this book, his parents were not recent immigrants to the United States. They emigrated from Germany in the

ALFRED STIEGLITZ

Taking Pictures, Making Painters

PHYLLIS ROSE

Jewish Lives

Alfred Stieglitz.

early nineteenth century. His father, a successful businessman, served as a lieutenant in the Union army.

Stieglitz attended Charlier Institute, a private school in New York City that prepared students for the Naval Academy, Harvard, Yale, Princeton and Columbia. In his junior year, his parents enrolled him in public high school so he would meet the qualifications to attend the CCNY, one of the few colleges at the time that accepted Jewish students. Stieglitz entered CCNY in 1880, attending the university for one academic year.

In 1881, Stieglitz's father sold his business and moved his family to Germany so his children could have a more challenging education than was available to them in the United States.

Initially interested in mechanical engineering, a subject made popular as industrialization was changing the world, Stieglitz shifted his focus to photography when he attended Technische Hochschule under the mentorship of Hermann Vogel.

In 1884, twenty-year-old Stieglitz bought his first camera and began taking pictures of peasant life and the European countryside. According to Stieglitz, photography "[f]ascinated me, first as a toy, then as a passion, then as an obsession." Known by many as the father of modern photography, Stieglitz's obsession would turn photographs into a fine art, and his photographs would establish street photography as a legitimate medium of that art. This was an unlikely legacy for a man who refused to sell his own photographs and faced insolvency more than once while building his reputation.

For the rest of the decade of the 1880s, Stieglitz supported himself by writing articles for the British magazine *Amateur Photographer* and entering photography contests, winning the magazine's Christmas photography contest.

After the death of his sister in 1890, Stieglitz returned to New York City to study photochemistry at the same time he founded the Photochrome Engraving Company, allowing him to pursue his interest and support himself. His interest would always be in the photographic processes, not in running the business.

That same year, Stieglitz formed the Camera Club of New York and published *Camera Notes*, a quarterly photographic journal published from 1903 through 1918 recognized as the finest photography magazine in the world.

After serving as editor of *Camera Notes*, Stieglitz published *Camera Work*, a forum for international modern art of all media. He was offered the position of co-editor of *American Amateur Photographer* but refused to accept a salary since Photochrome Engraving Company was printing the photographs for the periodical and Stieglitz did not want any appearance of a conflict of interest.

Alfred Stieglitz's famous photograph "The Steerage."

In 1896, Stieglitz combined the two major camera clubs in New York and formed the Camera Club of New York, accepting the position of vice-president, not president, again forgoing administrative responsibility to focus on photography as an art form.

With support of photographer Edward Steichen, in 1905 Stieglitz opened an exhibition space, the Little Galleries of the Photo-Secession,

Alfred Stieglitz official postage
stamp, 2002.

which later became known as Gallery 291. It was the first time paintings and photographs were exhibited on the same level for a showing.

In 1907, after he closed Gallery 291 for the summer, Stieglitz departed with his family to Paris as first-class passengers on SS *Kaiser Wilhelm II*. Although the first-class voyage was at the request of his wife, the discomfort Stieglitz felt being among the other first-class passengers was the impetus for him to take what would become one of the most important photographs of his career and in the history of photography, "The Steerage." The photograph is not only significant for the shapes and forms it captures but also for the message it conveys about its subjects, immigrants rejected at Ellis Island or returning to their old country. Stieglitz was so proud of "The Steerage" that he stated, "If it were all that survived of my body I would be pleased as I considered it a step in my evolution as a photographer."

In 1909, Stieglitz's father died, and he used his inheritance to keep Gallery 291 and *Camera Work* solvent. By 1917, with World War I and changes in the New York art world, Stieglitz could no longer afford to publish *Camera Work* or run Gallery 291. Although his business failed, this would be the year Stieglitz began work on the *Georgia O'Keeffe, A Portrait* series, which launched O'Keeffe's career and Stieglitz's tumultuous marriage to the famous modernist artist.

Stieglitz's bad luck in business would continue when in 1924 he opened a new gallery, the Intimate Gallery, which he nicknamed "The Room" because of its small size. The building that housed "The Room" was torn down in 1929. With funds raised by friends, he opened An American Place, the largest gallery he ever managed.

Stieglitz spent the last decades of his life devoted to running An American Place and taking photographs of the New York streetscape out of the gallery window. These final photographs solidified his position as the most significant figure in American photography.

Over the next years, Stieglitz experienced a series of heart attacks. In 1946, at the age of eighty-two, he suffered a fatal stroke. Over those eighty-two years, Stieglitz raised photography to an art form equal to painting, became known as the father of street photography and would forever be remembered as the man who shot what many consider the most important photograph in the history of photography, "The Steerage."

In 2002, the Masters of American Photography stamp series was issued by the U.S. Postal Service. The series honors twenty of the country's most important and influential photographers. Stieglitz's photo "Hands and Thimble" is included in this series.

William Klein

CCNY
ATTENDED 1940

William Klein was born in 1926 into an impoverished immigrant family. Living in an Irish neighborhood of New York City, he grew up surrounded by antisemitism. To quote Klein, "I was brought up on the streets. Part of a New York underclass." He summarized his contempt for New York City, saying, "New York is a monument to the dollar—the dollar is responsible for everything good and bad. Everybody comes for it. No one can resist it." Klein would use art to escape his surroundings and illustrate his disdain for New York.

Klein graduated from Townsend Harris High School* at fourteen and enrolled at CCNY to study sociology. At seventeen, after his father's clothing business failed and one year before graduation, Klein dropped out of CCNY and joined the U.S. Army, serving in Germany and France. During his military service, he drew cartoons for the military newspaper *Stars and Stripes*.

After being discharged from military service in 1948, his disdain for New York and its residents intact, Klein settled in Paris. Using his U.S. Army benefits, Klein enrolled in the Sorbonne. As a studio assistant of Fernand Leger, he developed an interest in abstract painting and sculpture.

---

* Townsend Harris founded the Free Academy of the City of New York in 1848 to provide education to the city's working people. The Free Academy would become CCNY. The introductory year of the Free Academy grew into Townsend Harris High School. The school was founded on traditions of scholarship and service to the community. In addition to William Klein, CCNY alumni including Ira Gershwin, Yip Harburg, Frank Loesser, Edward G. Robinson, Felix Frankfurter, Ben Ferencz and Jonas Salk, among others, would attend Townsend Harris.

William Klein.

Klein's breakthrough came when he was offered his first commission, to transfer the imagery from one of his paintings onto a series of movable wall panels for an interior designer. Early in life, Klein had won a camera in a poker game, and he experimented with what the camera allowed him to do. With this commission, Klein combined his fine art training and his experiments with photography.

In discussion with Rachel Small for *Interview Magazine* in 2013, Klein recalled this time of experimentation: "It was another kind of work with forms. I discovered that I could do whatever I wanted with a negative in a darkroom and an enlarger. I said, Hey I can say what I want about life around me, which I couldn't with these geometrical paintings."

In 1952, while exhibiting his abstract photographs in a gallery in Milan, Italy, a gallery visitor, Alexander Liberman, then art director of *Vogue*, saw in Klein's works the potential for fashion photography and offered Klein a job photographing for $100 per week, a significant amount of money at the time. Although he was not interested in fashion, Klein used this opportunity to introduce new techniques to fashion photography. His fashion photography would blur the lines between a critique of society and the classic beauty of the fashion model.

Klein moved back to New York City between 1955 and 1965. He photographed the people and places of New York City, putting models in

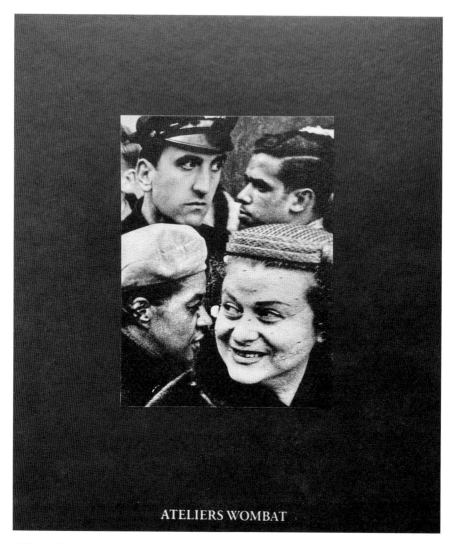

ATELIERS WOMBAT

William Klein's photograph "4 Heads, New York, 1954."

chaotic scenes of the city streets, and a new form of street photography was born. Klein shot the photographs that became the book *Life Is Good & Good for You in New York* over an eight-month period in 1956. *Vogue* rejected the photos in the book, seeing them as too critical a view of the city, and American publishers rejected the work as vulgar. The photographs included a Manhattan cityscape whose slow overexposure made the sunset look like Hiroshima at the moment of its atomic destruction.

"It seemed to me that blur gave another dimension to the lines, squares and circles we were all playing with and was a way out of the hard-edge rut," Klein told the author and curator Jane Livingston. "I was intrigued by what could be done with a camera." Klein won the Prix Nadar in 1957 for *Life Is Good & Good for You in New York.*

According to Martin Parr, "Klein took the language of tabloid newspapers, that very grainy black and white direct way of looking at the world I think coming back, he really smelled the energy of New York and wanted to translate that through these very grainy black and white, almost stream of consciousness images."

Following the success of *Life Is Good & Good for You in New York*, Klein photographed the streets of other cities, including Paris, Tokyo and Rome. His work was considered revolutionary for its rejection of the prevailing rules of photography. According to Jim Lewis in *Slate* magazine in 2003, "Klein broke half the rules of photography and ignored the other half."

From 1965 to the early 1980s, Klein abandoned photography and concentrated on film. The world of fashion became the subject for his first feature film, *Who Are You, Polly Maggoo?* (1966). Other films included *Far from Vietnam* (1967), protesting American involvement in the Vietnam War, and *Eldridge Cleaver, Black Panther* (1969), a sympathetic portrayal of the author and revolutionary who went into exile in Cuba and Algeria. Klein also produced more than 250 television commercials. His work was often openly critical of American society.

William Klein: YES, a retrospective, opened on June 3, 2022, at the International Center of Photographs. This was the first exhibit in his native city since 1994. "As usual, Mr. Klein rubs our faces in urban grime and dares us to be offended," photography critic Richard B. Woodward wrote in the *Times.*

William Klein died on September 12, 2022, at ninety-six as this profile was being written. His body of work elevated street photography to an art form while blurring the line between fashion photography and fine art. A new coffee table book paying tribute to the photographer will be published in 2023.

Garry Winogrand

CCNY
Attended 1947–1951

Born in 1928 to immigrant parents, Garry Winogrand grew up in a working-class area of the Bronx. His father was a leather worker in the garment industry, and his mother made neckties for piecemeal work.

In 1946, after graduating from high school, Winogrand entered the U.S. Army Air Force. While serving as a weather forecaster, he became interested in photography. Between 1947 and 1951, supported by the G.I. Bill, he studied painting at CCNY and photography at Columbia University.

But it was the scholarship Winogrand received to study photojournalism at the New School for Social Research that would influence his life's work. At the New School, he studied photojournalism under Alexey Brodovitch, who encouraged students to rely on instinct rather than science or methodological technique when photographing. This lesson was not lost on Winogrand.

In the 1950s and '60s, Winogrand supported himself as a freelance photojournalist and advertising photographer. During this time, though finding the work suffocating, he sold commercial photographs to magazines such as *Sports Illustrated*, *Collier's*, *Redbook*, *Life* and *Look*. In 1955, his work was included in the exhibition *The Family of Man*, curated by Edward Steichen, at the Museum of Modern Art in New York City.

By end of the 1950s, with television displacing magazines and photojournalism, Winogrand looked to the streets of New York to create photos of the human condition. He taught himself how to tilt his camera with a wide-angle lens, allowing him to include elements that would otherwise be cut off by the frame. The technique would change the face of street photography.

Critic Sean O'Hagan wrote in 2014, "In the 1960s and '70s Winogrand defined street photography as an attitude as well as a style—and it has labored in his shadow ever since so definitive are his photographs of New York."

During this period, Winogrand received three Guggenheim Fellowships, allowing him to pursue his work without financial concern: one in 1960 to explore "the effect of the media on events," one in 1964 to travel "for photographic studies of American life" and one in 1979 to travel throughout the southern and western United States investigating the social issues of his time.

In the 1970s, Winogrand taught in New York, Chicago and Texas while photographing high-profile events—including protests, press conferences, sports games, campaign rallies and museum openings—to capture what he

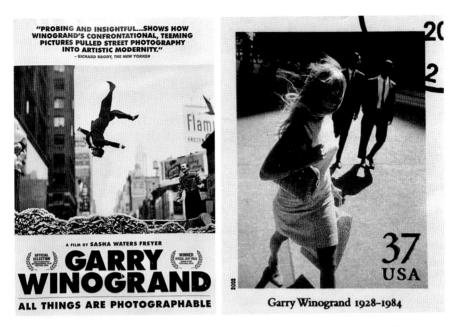

Left: Cover of the documentary *Garry Winogrand: All Things Are Photographable* (2018).

Right: Garry Winogrand official postage stamp, 2002.

called "the effect of the media on events" or the way people look and how they behave when they are participating in an event that will be reported in the media.

In 1975, at the height of the feminist revolution, Winogrand produced *Women Are Beautiful*, which explored his fascination with the female form. His timing, while it might have been intentional, could not have been worse. Many considered its publication a self-inflicted wound.

Winogrand, diagnosed with gallbladder cancer, died in 1984 at the age of fifty-six. At the time of his death, Winogrand left more than 2,500 rolls of film undeveloped and another 4,000 processed but not contact printed—in all, roughly one-third of a million frames.

In 2002, the Masters of American Photography stamp series was issued by the U.S. Postal Service. The series honors twenty of the country's most important and influential photographers. Winogrand's "Photograph of Pedestrian" is included in this series.

In 2013, the first major retrospective of his work in twenty-five years was held at the San Francisco Museum of Modern Art, exhibiting nearly one hundred photos that the photographer himself had never seen.

Ben Shahn

CCNY
BA, 1924

Ben Shahn, one of the most significant social critics among painters of the twentieth century, was born in 1898 in Kovno, Lithuania. At five years old, his childhood ended when his father was sentenced to Siberia. The Shahn family immigrated to America via Sweden and South Africa in 1906 after his father escaped imprisonment. By this time, the seeds of Ben Shahn's social conscience and his artistic legacy had been planted. Yet from the start, the road Shahn traveled was beset with rejection and controversy.

Shahn's early education in Lithuania was in Hebrew school, where in addition to Hebrew he learned Yiddish and Russian. This was of little help when he entered school in Brooklyn. According to Shahn, "As soon as I got to America, I was put into school not knowing a word of the English language. An uncle took me to show me a department store and bought me a xylophone. The next day I took it to school, and the teacher was furious. She said, 'Where did you get this?' And I said, 'My uncle bought it for me,' and I said, 'I haven't seen him for 25 years.' I meant to say weeks, but I didn't know the word. She took me to another class, and I was put into an idiot class." Drawing would be Shahn's salvation.

Everything changed when Shahn entered fifth grade. "A remarkable thing happened. I had a teacher by the name of Miss Quick. She saw and knew about my drawing. She bought me with her own money watercolors and crayons and put me off in the corner of the room and told me to draw." Shahn's only question to her was, "How do I ever get into sixth grade?" His teacher replied, "I will teach you everything you have to know in a week before you go into sixth grade." One year after being loaned to other teachers to draw Santa Clauses and turkeys for Thanksgiving, Shahn received his first paid art job writing names on graduation diplomas, the first time a student was given this honor.

When he was fourteen, his mother insisted he drop out of high school and work to help support his family. He became an apprentice to his uncle, a lithographer. Shahn continued his education, taking night classes and art classes at the Educational Alliance on New York's Lower East Side. In 1917, he completed his apprenticeship, left his uncle's shop and continued to do freelance lithography work. At nineteen, Shahn was a professional lithographer.

Ben Shahn.

By the fall of 1919, Shahn had earned enough money to pursue a college education and enrolled at NYU as a biology major. Although an honors student, he changed direction, considered a career as an artist and transferred to CCNY, where he studied between 1921 and 1924. After graduation, Shahn enrolled at the National Academy of Design for two years, followed by travel in Europe and North Africa. He eventually settled in Paris, where he studied French at the Sorbonne and art at the Acadamie de la Grande Chaumiere.

Shahn returned to America in 1929 and had his first one-man show of the watercolors and oil paintings he completed while in Europe. Despite this success, Shahn was dissatisfied with the work inspired by his travels. "Here I am, I said to myself, 32 years old, the son of a carpenter, I like stories and people. The French school is not for me." Shahn wanted to make what he called social communication with his art. Two events would provide him with the opportunity to achieve his goals.

The first event was the 1931 trial of two immigrant workmen, Nicola Sacco and Bartolomeo Vanzetti, who were accused of murdering a paymaster and were eventually executed. The Sacco and Vanzetti trial allowed Shahn, through a series of gouache paintings, to comment on the plight of immigrants, labor radicalism and economic inequality. When Shahn submitted his Sacco and Vanzetti paintings to an exhibition at the New York Museum of Modern Art, the museum's board of trustees objected to one painting depicting the committee that denied Sacco and Vanzetti's appeal. The committee members were friends with many of the museum's trustees. Despite the board's demand that Shahn's works not be shown, the other artists in the exhibition and the curator refused to participate if Shahn (and two other artists) was banned. The MOMA show moved forward, including Shahn's work, resulting in many of the trustees resigning in anger.[*]

Spurred on by the Sacco and Vanzetti controversy, Shahn followed with a series of paintings on the 1932 bombing trial of labor leader Tom Mooney. This led to the second pivotal event in Shahn's career when, in 1933, the Mooney series caught the interest of Mexican mural painter Diego Rivera. Rivera asked Shahn to assist him on a mural project for the RCA building at Rockefeller Center. Again, controversy and rejection followed when the Rockefeller Center project was canceled because the mural included a portrait of Lenin. The unfinished painting was covered with little canvases to hide it from view and was destroyed the following year.

After the cancelation of the Rockefeller Center project, Shahn began a series of tempera studies for a mural on Prohibition for the Publics Works of Art Project (PWAP). The design was rejected by the Municipal Art Commission and never executed. This rejection propelled Shahn to again change his creative path.

_____

[*] Two other CCNY alumni profiled in this book, Felix Frankfurter and Upton Sinclair, also used their respective platforms to expose the injustice of the Sacco and Vanzetti affair.

Ben Shahn's famous painting *The Passion of Sacco and Vanzetti*.

Shahn decided to document his paintings through photography. His intention was to use his photographs as well as ones he clipped from newspapers as course materials for his paintings, graphics and murals. Without the resources to buy a camera, Shahn made a deal with his brother to buy him a 35mm Leica camera for twenty-five dollars with the promise that he would give back the money if he failed to get a photo published from the first roll of film he took. Shahn won the bet when, in 1934, a photo of a theater group performing on a New York City sidewalk was published in *New Theater*, a radical arts magazine. What followed were thousands of photographs, black-and-whites of New York City and its residents. The photographs documented the poor, immigrant and neglected neighborhoods of the city and the lives he saw desperately in need of help. Art as social commentary had found a home in Ben Shahn's photography.

In 1935, when the Roosevelt administration and the Farm Securities Administration (FSA) set out to prove to the American voter and to members of Congress that there was poverty that required immediate legislative attention, Shahn was hired to document rural poverty in America through photography. (Shahn was later commissioned to take a second set of photographs to illustrate the positive impact of those government programs approved by Congress.) Between 1935 and 1938, when he resigned, Shahn traveled through the South and Midwest documenting American small-town culture with his 35mm Leica camera. It was Shahn's first exposure to the United States outside of New York. By the end of the project, Shahn had produced more than six thousand photographs for the FSA, many of them now in the Library of Congress. Shahn's art as social commentary finally found its place in the American landscape. Or so it seemed.

In 1938, Shahn painted *Resources in America*, a commissioned mural completed for the Bronx Central Post Office in New York City. Selected as a winning design by the New Deal's Treasury Section of Painting and Sculpture, it elicited harsh criticism due to the inclusion of a quote by Whitman, who was then on the Catholic Church's "Index of Forbidden Books and Authors." Because Shahn agreed when taking the job to make changes if there were objections, he changed the text. This experience was not the first nor would it be the last to remind Shahn of the power that a few members of the public could exert over an artist's work.

In 1942, Shahn began work for the Office of War Information designing posters and pamphlets. He left a year later. Only two of the posters Shahn

Ben Shahn official postage stamp, 1998.

designed were published. With this rejection, Shahn turned from public works to commercial work and from social realism to what he called personal realism. His art became less about society and more personal and symbolic. Shahn summed up his contribution to raising the quality of commercial art: "I never let out a thing until I would be as happy with it hanging in a museum or reproduced in the *Daily News*. I don't care where."

Despite negative reviews by critics, Shahn's realist works had broad public appeal. In 1947, Shahn became the youngest artist to have a retrospective at the New York Museum of Modern Art, the same museum that a decade earlier had objected to his Sacco and Vanzetti paintings. In 1948, Shahn was named one of the ten leading American painters in a *Look* magazine poll of museum directors.

Controversy continued to shadow Shahn. In 1959, during McCarthy's House Un-American Activities Committee (HUAC) hearings, Shahn refused to testify before members of the committee. According to *Art Story*, "The FBI maintained an active file on Shahn up until his death."

In 1961, Shahn was awarded the Contemporary American Oil Paintings Exhibition Medal by the Corcoran Gallery in Washington, D.C. In 1964, he was awarded the National Institute of Arts and Letters Gold Medal from the American Academy of Arts and Letters.

Shahn's painting *18th Amendment Prohibition Enforced* graces the face of a U.S. postage stamp. The painting, showing federal agents disposing of wine, hangs in the Museum of the City of New York.

Until his death in 1969, Ben Shahn considered himself "a worker engaged with society, not an elite artist set apart from it. His subjects were the social outcasts who were not welcome at the museums and were not the traditional subjects of museum art." Rejection and controversy notwithstanding.

Ralph Lauren

CCNY
Attended 1957–1960

The life of Ralph Lauren, a man with an estimated net worth of more than $7 billion, is considered one of the greatest reinvention stories of all times. This story began in the Bronx in 1939, when Ralph Lifshitz, the youngest of four children, was born to immigrants from Belarus. The Lifshitz family lived in a two-bedroom apartment where Lauren shared one bedroom with his two older brothers. His parents spoke broken English. Their neighbors were all immigrants.

Lauren's father was a house painter but aspired to be a fine artist. He never said he was a painter. He said he was an interior decorator. To make a living, his father painted neighborhood apartments when people moved out. According to Lauren, "I came from nowhere. I had nothing.…I grew up sleeping three to a room, the shortest kid in my class, with a lisp and a lazy eye."

As a child, Lauren wanted to be a professional basketball player. His mother wanted him to be a rabbi. For two and a half years from kindergarten to second grade, Lauren attended PS 80. In 1947, his mother insisted that he enter Yeshiva Hebrew School, where students studied holy texts during the day and English subjects for an hour each afternoon. As a Yeshiva student, Lauren received an A in art but did not do as well in other subjects. Lauren would not become the rabbi his mother wished. But according to childhood friends, Lauren did meet his mother's second wish—that he be well dressed.

In the fall of 1950, Lauren left Yeshiva and returned to PS 80. At the age of twelve, he began working after school selling handmade ties to his fellow students. His family didn't have a TV, so he went to the home of his friends and watched TV series like *Hopalong Cassidy* that emphasized positive values, heroism and patriotism. Lauren would spend his afternoons at the movies, imagining the elegant life he saw on the screen embodied by actors like Cary Grant and Fred Astaire. These themes of heroism, patriotism and elegance would find themselves in the fashions Lauren would design and the philanthropies he would support decades later.

The year Lauren turned thirteen, his mother "pulled the rug out from under his life" and sent him back to Yeshiva for a year to graduate and become a rabbi. On June 22, 1953, Ralph Lifshitz was among the fifty-four Yeshiva graduates. That September, he entered Manhattan Talmudical

Ralph Lauren.

Academy. On the application, he wrote that he was the captain of the Yeshiva basketball team. No one noticed that Yeshiva did not have a basketball team.

In 1954, at the start of tenth grade, Lauren dropped out of the academy and transferred to DeWitt Clinton High School. His religious education was over. He did not want to be a rabbi. He wanted to be Mickey Mantle or a teacher or a movie star or an artist, although he felt that he wasn't handsome enough, tall enough or talented enough. This was the same year that one of Lauren's older brothers, a reservist in the U.S. Air Force, grew tired of humorous mispronunciations of his last name at roll call and changed his and Ralph's last name. Ralph Lifshitz became Ralph Lauren.

Lauren graduated from DeWitt Clinton High School in 1957. His yearbook noted his desire to become a millionaire and predicted that he would be attending CCNY.

In the fall of 1957, Ralph Lifshitz enrolled as Ralph Lauren in Baruch College at CCNY, where he studied business. But CCNY, a commuter school, was not Lauren's idea of the college campus he had seen portrayed on the silver screen. He attended school until, one day, he asked himself why he was studying business when he could be doing business.

Lauren switched to night classes and took a job at Allied Stores, a department store where employees known as buyers scoured the garment district seeking out manufacturers and ordering clothing for retail stores. He was called an assistant furnishings buyer, but he was really a clerk. The pay was low, but enough to buy clothing he loved for himself. Lauren still lived at home and didn't have to pay rent.

At first, Lauren liked the business world, but the more he learned about Allied Stores, the less he wanted a life in business, a life he saw as lacking integrity. He preferred to be in school and on campus. He wanted to be a teacher and wear tweed jackets. In reality, what Lauren wanted was to live in the idealized version of academia he saw on the silver screen as a teenager. He returned to CCNY during the day only to again be disappointed. In June 1960, at the end of his third year, he quit CCNY.

After dropping out of CCNY and waiting to be drafted, Lauren was hired by Brooks Brothers as its youngest sales assistant at sixty-five dollars per week. He was responsible for the mid-priced neck ware counter. He loved the all-American look of Brooks Brothers, but it represented yesterday's fashion.

In 1960, Lauren was drafted and served as a supply clerk in the U.S. Army Reserves. Again, he was disillusioned when the reality of the army fell short of its slogan—"Join the Army and See the World." According to Lauren, in the army "[y]ou have no face. You're not a person. You're a robot." The world he had spent his young life trying to escape.

At twenty-two, after dropping out of college and serving in the army, Lauren moved back into his childhood bedroom and found a job as a shipping clerk at a glove company, Meyers Make. Eventually, he rose to salesman. But like Brooks Brothers, Lauren saw Meyers Make as the last decade. Ralph Lauren wanted to be the next decade.

A series of dead-end jobs followed. The first job was at Daniel Hays, where Lauren earned a 6 percent commission selling gloves and a 10 percent commission selling fragrances. Next Lauren sold ties for A. Rivitz and Company, where he was allowed to develop his own wide tie designs. Only a few customers were interested, and Lauren quit before his ties were replaced with more traditional inventory.

Lauren was twenty-eight when he decided to create his own line—"a business that was going to be the new Brooks Brothers." He would start small with what he knew: ties. But he needed to obtain credit and find someone to back his business. Enter Ned Brower of Beau Brummell, a manufacturer of ties that were the antithesis of Lauren's vison.

Despite the difference of styles, Lauren convinced Brower to let him start his own line. Lauren was given a single drawer in the Empire State Building. He would have to do everything himself—purchasing, designing, selling and shipping—but Ralph Lauren now had his own line. The Ralph Lauren Corporation started in 1967, selling men's ties under the name Polo. Ralph Lauren would spend the next fifty years building his tie business into a global brand.

Ralph Lauren's ties were four to four and a half inches wide. They were elegant, and they were expensive—$7.50 to $15 apiece at a time when the most expensive ties sold for $5 each. Lauren's first client, Paul Stuart, agreed to sell his ties but not with the Polo label. Bloomingdale's would only sell his ties if Lauren replaced his Polo label with one from the store and reduced their width by one-quarter inch. Lauren refused to compromise. His first

"The Star-Spangled Banner," immortalized by Francis Scott Key in the American national anthem, restored with generous support from Ralph Lauren in 1998–99 and housed at the Smithsonian in Washington, D.C.

break came when Neiman Marcus ordered 1,200 ties. Lauren sold $500,000 worth of ties his first year in business. Six months later, Bloomingdale's was back, without conditions.

Buoyed by his initial success and the backing from New York clothing manufacturer Norman Hilton, Lauren expanded into a full menswear collection. He started designing shirts and then suits. "In those days, a shirt company made shirts, a tie company made ties," Lauren said, "but I made them all. That was a radical thing." And it was a success.

In 1971, less than five years after creating his first tie, Lauren expanded his line, creating his first women's collection and opening a Polo boutique on Rodeo Drive, making him the first American designer with a freestanding store. This would be one of the many firsts for Ralph Lauren. Along the way, Lauren became the genius behind aspirational lifestyle marketing.

In 1974, Ralph Lauren designed Robert Redford's wardrobe for his character in *The Great Gatsby*, and he was the first designer to be featured in his own advertising campaign. In 1977, Diane Keaton and Woody Allen wore his clothing in the movie *Annie Hall*.

In 1978, Ralph Lauren fragrances produced by Warner Brothers, Lauren LTD, were launched at Bloomingdale's. This was the first time that a designer introduced two fragrances, one for men and one for women, simultaneously.

In 1981, Ralph Lauren opened the first freestanding store for an American designer in London's West End, on Northwest Bond Street.

Ralph Lauren was one of the first major designers to expand his brand into homewares and the first fashion designer to design a full home collection. He is the only designer to win the Council of Fashion Designers of America (CFDA) four times.

Like all rags-to-riches stories, Lauren's success is also a story of deals gone wrong and how he managed to pull the company from the brink of financial disaster more than once. Lauren learned from these experiences, and on June 12, 1997, Polo Ralph Lauren became a publicly traded company on the New York Stock Exchange. The company now has more than 450 global stores. Ralph Lauren currently controls 84 percent of the voting rights of the company, making him, as of 2015, the single richest fashion designer in the world. To quote Oprah Winfrey, "All by selling the life you'd like to lead and by offering a snapshot of a storybook lifestyle that somehow feels attainable."

Ralph Lifshitz's story is "about how a first-generation American tie salesman became the embodiment of the American dream." Ralph Lauren's story is "about a marketing genius whose brand conjures Ivy League privilege yet made billions from expensive polo shirts."

To cap the American dream that his life and his business personify, in 1999 Lauren financed the restoration of the original "Star-Spangled Banner" flag now on display at the Smithsonian.

Chapter 2
BUSINESS AND EDUCATION

Jean Nidetch

CCNY
Attended 1942

Jean Nidetch died at 142, her goal weight. Anyone of the 5 million people who today belong to Weight Watchers can relate to this. What many people don't know is that the story of Weight Watchers began not with Oprah but with Jean.

Jean Nidetch née Slutsky, the daughter of a nail stylist and a taxi driver, was born in Brooklyn, New York, in 1923. Her father sold sandwiches and coffee to work gangs to earn extra money during the Depression. Her mother helped by making the sandwiches. According to Nidetch, "I'm sure that my compulsive eating habits began when I was a baby....Whenever I cried, my mother gave me something to eat." And so began a lifelong struggle with food, or so she thought.

Nidetch attended Girls High School in Bedford and was popular among her friends, all of whom were plus-sized.* "We all felt that thin people were different because it seemed they could eat anything they wanted and not gain weight."

---

* Plus-sized clothing was introduced by Lane Bryant in the early 1920s to fill an unaddressed clothing niche. The term "plus-sized" officially entered the fashion lexicon in the 1970s with the introduction of models who wore larger than a size 10, equivalent to a size 6 today.

Jean Nidetch in an advertisement for Weight Watchers.

Although she earned a partial scholarship to Long Island University because her parents could not afford the remaining tuition, Nidetch attended CCNY, where she majored in business administration. When her father died unexpectedly in 1942, she dropped out to support her mother.

Nidetch's first job was working for ten dollars a week at a furniture store. She then worked for Man O'War Publishing Company, where she produced tip sheets for horse players until Mayor La Guardia's campaign against horse racing put the company out of business. Her next job was at the Internal Revenue Service, where she met her future husband, Mortimer Nidetch, a bus driver.

In 1945, Nidetch began a courtship with her prospective husband that was all about food and finding new places to eat. After two years of "diner hopping," she married her eating companion. While raising two sons, she helped support the family by selling eggs door to door for her aunt, who owned a chicken farm in nearby New Jersey. Nidetch soon realized that everyone in her life was overweight, her eating habits were compulsive and no one seemed to notice or care. She described herself as "an overweight housewife obsessed with eating cookies." At thirty-eight years old and five-foot-seven, Nidetch weighed 214 pounds.

The breaking point came in 1961, when Nidetch was mistaken for a pregnant woman while shopping in a grocery store, a story she would repeat many times. "I remember the day vividly. It was October 1961. I woke up that morning and I was having a 'thin day.' Did you know you can weigh 214 lbs. and have a thin day? Of course! You just get up and you're thin! As I was walking in and out of the aisles, I met a lady that I had met before…she said, 'Jean! You look so wonderful.' And I thought to myself 'She is noticing. I'm thin!' And then she said, 'When are you due?'"

Nidetch immediately enrolled in a free ten-week weight loss program sponsored by the New York City Board of Health's obesity clinic. Little did Nidetch know that this course would change the meaning of the word *diet* not just for her but for millions of people around the world. The program was called the "Prudent Diet" and included the dictums, "No skipping meals. Fish five times a week. Two pieces of bread and two glasses of skim milk a day. More fruits and vegetables and eating liver once a week." It prohibited alcohol, sweets and fatty foods. The diet included a list of allowed foods and the quantities allowed and encouraged weighing portions.

Although Nidetch lost twenty pounds on the ten-week program, she was unhappy that the program administrator discouraged conversation. Challenged by her habit of hiding and eating Mallomars cookies, she began a weekly support group in her home. Initially, she invited six overweight friends. Within two months, the weekly group had grown to forty women. Nidetch introduced the "Prudent Diet" to the group, while the members provided support to one another coupled with weekly weigh-ins, a reward system for each 10 pounds lost and prizes for reaching weight-loss milestones. Nidetch charged twenty-five cents to cover her cost for the meeting. By

October 1962, Nidetch had reached her goal weight of 142 pounds, a loss of 72 pounds. Her husband had lost 70 pounds and her mother 57 pounds. The secret to Nidetch's success was a combination of diet, exercise and, most importantly, psychology.

Interest in Nidetch's meetings spread to other neighborhoods, where groups started to form. One group was at the home of Al and Felice Lippert—Al a CCNY alumni and Felice a Hunter College alumna. After successfully losing weight, Mr. Lippert, a businessman in the garment industry, convinced Nidetch that she could make a business out of her weight-loss support groups. Lippert offered his business expertise and financial backing. Felice Lippert oversaw nutrition, food research and recipe development. Weight Watchers was born.

Nidetch and Lippert rented an old theater in Little Neck, New York, charged participants two dollars per week (the same cost as a movie) and hired successful participants as guest lecturers. Nidetch was shocked when four hundred people arrived at the first meeting. In 1966, the first Weight Watchers cookbook was published, selling more than 1 million copies. Eventually, Weight Watchers was franchised, and branches opened across the country.

In 1968, six years after Nidetch reached her goal weight, Weight Watchers became a publicly traded company. In 1973, the company's tenth anniversary, at fifty years old, Nidetch stepped down as president; in 1978, Weight Watchers was sold to H.J. Heinz Company for close to $71 million. Nidetch walked away with $7 million ($31.4 million in today's dollars).

Although officially retired, Nidetch remained the face and story of Weight Watchers. By 1986, there were eighty-one franchises in forty-three states and ten overseas locations, proving that the desire to reach your goal weight has no boundaries.

With competition in the weight-loss business in the '80s and '90s, Heinz Company developed frozen meals called Weight Watchers Smart Ones. The system of counting and weighing food that was part of Nidetch's original success story was replaced with the POINTS system, "an algorithmic formula that quantifies a food portion based on carbohydrates, fat and fiber content." In 1984, a series of ambassadors, beginning with Lynn Redgrave, replaced Nidetch as the spokeswoman for Weight Watchers. In 1997, after being labeled the "Duchess of Pork" by the media, Sarah Ferguson, the former wife of Prince Andrew, lost close to eighty pounds and became the face (and figure) of the company. In 1999, Weight Watchers was sold again, this time for $735 million. In 2001, the website weightwatchers.

Cover of Nidetch's best-selling memoir.

com was launched. Seven years later, Weight Watchers for Men was established.

Nidetch's positive influence on millions of people around the world was acknowledged in 1989, when she won the Horatio Alger Award, an award conferred on ten to twelve individuals each year who symbolize the values of personal initiative, perseverance, leadership, commitment to excellence, belief in the free enterprise system and the importance of higher education, community service and the vision and determination to achieve a better future. In winning this award, Nidetch joined other CCNY alumni like Bernard Baruch, Colin Powell, E.Y. Harburg and Henry Kissinger, as well as Weight Watchers spokesperson Oprah Winfrey and competitor Jenny Craig.

In her acceptance speech, Nidetch reflected on Weight Watchers and what it meant to her and others who stood in similar shoes. "To be recognized as an obese person by society in a meaningful way was more than I could have ever hoped for, as small groups of us gathered in our communities and discovered that together we are strong. We learned to alter our eating habits and our lives changed forever. We no longer suffered with the handicap of obesity. In dignity, with perseverance and with passion for each other, with patience and with determination, we reached our goals and became as one member of Weight Watchers told me, 'part of the human race.'"

Jean Nidetch died in 2015, the same year Oprah Winfrey bought a 10 percent stake in the company. The purchase generated $700 million in stock market value in two days. But Oprah's endorsement was not enough to surmount competition in the weight-loss market from companies like Jenny Craig and Nutrisystem. In 2018, Weight Watchers rebranded itself as WW International, refocusing on the psychological and health components of weight loss that Nidetch had emphasized fifty-five years earlier.

As this profile is being written, WW International joins the prescription weight-loss drug business with the $106 million acquisition of Sequence, a tele-help subscription service that connects patients with doctors who can prescribe weight-loss drugs.

Stanley Kaplan

CCNY
BA, 1939
MSE, 1941

Stanley Kaplan sold hope to millions of students excluded from a higher education system based on privilege rather than hard work. But in his quest, Kaplan became a pariah in education circles.

Stanley Kaplan was born in Brooklyn in 1921 to eastern European immigrant parents with limited formal education but a determination that their children would attend college. His mother lined the basement of the family home with books that Kaplan turned into a lending library when he was seven years old. He issued library cards to neighborhood children, monitored checkouts and returns and charged a late fee of one penny a week for each book. It was from this backdrop that a billion-dollar industry would be born.

According to Kaplan in his autobiography, *Test Pilot*, "While other children played doctor, I played teacher. If my friends complained about math fractions and percents, I would sit down with pencil and paper and explain to them how to solve the problem." Sometimes Kaplan would offer them a dime if they just sat and listened to him.

When his father did not recover from the bankruptcy of his plumbing business during the Great Depression, Kaplan worked odd jobs to support his family. But this did not stop him from skipping two grades while continuing to tutor his friends. Kaplan was such a good tutor that a story began to circulate: when the grades of a student he tutored went from failing to an A, the student was accused of cheating.

Kaplan's skill in tutoring did not go unnoticed by his school's employment counselor, who made him an offer that changed his life. The school would pay him twenty-five cents per hour to help failing students. Kaplan would soon have ten paying students. He was fourteen years old.

When Kaplan graduated high school in 1935 at sixteen years old, his dream was to attend Columbia University, but his family could not afford the tuition. Instead, he attended CCNY after receiving a scholarship based on his scores on the New York State Regents Examination.

According to Kaplan about CCNY, "When I wasn't studying, I was tutoring students. When I wasn't tutoring, I was studying hard and making great grades. My successes as both tutor and student gave me all the confidence I needed to keep pace with my older college peers."

Kaplan received straight As at CCNY until his sophomore year, when he received a C in biology, which he believed was his best subject. When he questioned his professor about the grade, he found that there was another Stanley Kaplan in the class and *that* Stanley Kaplan had received the C grade. Kaplan adopted Henry as his middle name, and Stanley H. Kaplan was born to avoid future confusion. For the rest of his life, when asked what the "H" stood for, he answered, "Higher scores, of course!"

Stanley Kaplan.

During his junior year at CCNY, Kaplan applied to medical school. He was Phi Beta Kappa and ranked no. 2 in his 1939 CCNY graduating class. He applied to five New York City medical schools and was rejected by all five. Reflecting on his disappointment, Kaplan said, "Failure was as foreign to me as a trip outside New York City, and the news came as a humbling defeat. My Jewish friends at private colleges such as Columbia and Harvard had been accepted by medical schools. And my non-Jewish friends at City College were accepted at medical schools. Soon I made the connection: I was Jewish, and I attended a public college."

With medical school out of reach, Kaplan committed himself to teaching neighborhood youngsters in the basement room of his parents' house, the same room where he had started a lending library as a child. He put a sign outside the house reading "Stanley H. Kaplan Educational Center" and began tutoring one hundred students to prepare for the New York State Regents Exam. Word spread that Stanley Kaplan could help you get into college. Stanley H. Kaplan Educational Center was becoming the impoverished student's prep school.

As part of his tutoring, Kaplan purchased Barron's study guides and answer keys published by Manuel Barron and sold in Barron's New York City bookstore. When Kaplan pointed out errors in the study guides to Barron, Barron offered him a job writing and editing the New York Regents Exam answer guides. Kaplan wrote sixteen answer guides, claiming that "it was a great way to promote my tutoring business and give me exposure in the education and publishing world."

In 1946, a high school student asked Kaplan for help on an exam he was unfamiliar with called the Scholastic Aptitude Test (SAT). The SAT instructions stated that the test was a measure of a student's innate intelligence and not learned knowledge and advised students not to prepare for the test. Ignoring the SAT instructions, Kaplan helped the student with math and reading comprehension, and she easily passed the exams. According to Malcolm Gladwell, "From that moment forward the business of getting into college in America would never quite be the same."

In proving that the SAT was coachable, Kaplan had undermined the unspoken use of aptitude tests to address what Ivy League school administrators labeled the "Jewish problem." Between World War I and World War II, there was an unwritten policy of Ivy League schools to limit the admittance of children of eastern European immigrants, especially Jews, who were deemed "underliving and overworking" by school administrators. For example, Columbia University policy required applicants to take an aptitude test for admission in addition to the New York State Regents Exam. According to Herbert Hawkes, the dean of Columbia College during this period, "because the typical Jewish student was simply a 'grind' who excelled on the Regents Exams because he worked so hard, a test of innate intelligence would put him back in his place. We prefer naturals to grinds...we think that people who achieve based on vast reserves of innate ability are somehow more promising and more worthy than those who simply work hard."*

By helping students who would otherwise not have a chance for admittance to the Ivy League study for aptitude tests like the SAT, Kaplan proved that practice, not privilege, was the best measure of academic success.

With the passage of the G.I. Bill and the onslaught of World War II veterans applying to college, the demand for Kaplan's help became too large for him to continue running his business from his parents' basement. In 1951, Kaplan opened his first standalone school. Within a decade, he had seventeen centers offering tutoring for a variety of tests.

Students knew that Kaplan courses worked, but educators and test makers continued to think that test preparation was tantamount to cheating. To quote Kaplan, "I believed I was offering a quality service the students wanted and needed, so I was disappointed when fellow educators criticized me and excluded me from their meetings." Many educators claimed that Kaplan was just trying to advance his business and earn a profit "by preying

---

* This is little different from the policy being challenged today in the courts that limits the number of hardworking Asian students from admittance to Ivy League schools.

Cover of the 1994 Kaplan SAT prep book.

on students' anxieties." To this, he replied, "But I didn't create the anxieties, I just tried to ease them."

As Kaplan's success grew, criticism of his tutoring schools escalated. In 1957, the College Board put out a statement that called tutoring services/test prep a waste of time and money. Kaplan responded, "To say you can't improve scores is to say you can't improve students, and I disagree with that."

The denunciation of tutoring services culminated in 1979, when the Federal Trade Commission launched an investigation into the test prep industry and found that preparation for college prep exams can raise students' scores by an average of 25 points, not the 100 points that Kaplan claimed in his advertisements. But 25 points was enough. By this time, Stanley H. Kaplan Educational Testing Centers had grown to eighty-four locations with thirty thousand students.

The Educational Testing Service (ETS) that creates the SAT continued to assume that the SAT was uncoachable and that increasing one's score could only be accomplished by illegitimate means—the most recent college admittance scandal, "Varsity Blues," notwithstanding. Despite the never-ending controversy, Kaplan would continue to proclaim his love for the SAT, a test he thought gave people like him the best chance of overcoming discrimination. It was not until 1983 that Kaplan's relationship with the educational establishment would take a turn for the better when he was asked to speak at the College Board's annual conference. He viewed this as one of the highlights of his life.

In 1984, Stanley H. Kaplan Company was sold for $45 million ($128.9 million in today's dollars) to the Washington Post Company. By the time it was sold, it had expanded to more than one hundred centers nationally, six hundred part-time satellite offices and ninety-five thousand students per year. The acquisition transformed Washington Post into an education and media company.

Kaplan stayed with the company until 1994, serving as the president and director of the Rita J. and Stanley H. Kaplan Family Foundation. Kaplan retired at seventy-four after devoting fifty-six years to education.

In August 2009, Kaplan died of a heart attack at the age of ninety.

To the end, Kaplan considered himself "a poor man's private school," providing access to higher education for millions of students based on effort, not aptitude. As his obituary put it, "This all from the simple idea that you can actually study for the SAT."

ANDREW GROVE

CCNY
BS, 1960

He endured the Nazi occupation and Communist rule of Hungary, overcame the loss of his hearing and survived Parkinson's disease and prostate cancer. Andrew "Andy" Grove personifies the maxim "only the paranoid survive," which he coined as the driving force behind Intel Corporation, one of the most admired companies in the world.

Grove was born András István Gróf on September 2, 1936, in Budapest, Hungary. His father, with little formal education, taught himself business accounting and ran a small dairy business. While the Gróf family rose to the middle class through hard work, the economic success of the family did not shield their son from personal hardship.

At four years old, Grove contracted scarlet fever and nearly died. After a long hospital stay, he returned home partially deaf. Grove never learned ASL nor did he live as a person who was hearing impaired. Grove never wanted his deafness known, always afraid that people would take advantage of what they might perceive as a weakness.

In 1944, when the Nazis overthrew the Hungarian government, Grove's father was taken by German troops and sent to a labor camp, where he survived torture, typhoid and pneumonia. Grove and his mother were hidden by a Christian family until the end of the war, when the family was reunited. While in hiding, Grove's mother changed their names to conceal their identities. According to Grove, "I was eight years old, and I knew bad things were happening, but I don't remember the details. My mother took me away. She explained to me what it meant that I would have a different name, that I cannot make a mistake, that I had to forget my name and that I couldn't, if they said, 'Write your name,' I couldn't write it down." András István Gróf became Andras Malesevics.

Any hope that the Gróf family had of returning to their prewar life was short-lived with the domination of the postwar Hungarian government by the Communist Party. This was acutely felt by Grove when at fourteen he joined a

Andrew Grove's *TIME* Man of the Year cover from 1998.

local youth newspaper as a reporter. Soon disillusioned by the so-called facts that he was reporting, Grove recalled, "I did not want a profession in which a totally subjective evaluation, easily colored by political considerations, could decide the merits of my work. I ran from writing to science."

In 1956, with the Hungarian uprising, Grove ran again, this time to America with his best friend Janos Lanyi. Grove and Lanyi crossed the border into Austria, crawling in mud to evade Soviet soldiers. With help from the International Rescue Committee, Grove and Lanyi boarded a refugee ship to New York City, where they stayed in a former prisoner of war camp in New Jersey until they could obtain the proper paperwork to remain in America.

Grove eventually moved to the Bronx to live with his aunt and uncle, who had immigrated to the United States in the 1930s. He Americanized his name, and for the first time in his life, Andy Grove could write his name without fear.

In 1957, Grove enrolled at CCNY with a major in mechanical engineering. His hearing impairment, compounded by his limited command of English, made classwork difficult. Not deterred, he learned how to read lips to overcome his hearing loss. And after class he would go to the library and decipher his class notes with a dictionary by his side. In 1960, Grove graduated at the top of his class. To quote Grove's advisor, Morris Kolodney, "I was a little astonished by that kind of ambition. There's some advantage in being hungry."

After graduation, Grove moved to California and in 1963 earned a doctorate in chemical engineering from the University of California–Berkeley. Subsequently, he was hired by Fairchild Semiconductor Research Laboratory to lead a research team that worked on transistors and silicon wafers.

In 1968, Grove's bosses at Fairchild Semiconductor, Robert Noyce and Gordon Moore, founded a new company, Intel, that supplied memory chips for mainframe computers. The two-man operation became a team of three when they recruited Grove as an employee.

At Intel, Grove oversaw factory production. In his quest to surpass Intel's competition, Grove became the founding father of Intel's philosophy of "creative confrontation"—it is better to scream at one another and come to a solution quickly than to let issues fester over time. According to Grove's successor, Craig Barrett, Andy's goal was "to hit you over the head with a two-by-four."

Andrew Grove official postage stamp from Palau, 1999.

His management style notwithstanding, Grove's success at Intel was undeniable. Because of his insight, Intel moved from memory chips to microprocessors, and as a result, by 2004, Intel's microprocessors powered 80 to 90 percent of all personal computers. Those of us of a certain age will remember hearing the slogan "Intel Inside" when turning on just about any personal computer during the first decade of the twenty-first century.

Grove advanced from production manager to president and then CEO and chairman of the board of Intel. In addition to his groundbreaking work at Intel, Grove authored seven books. In *Only the Paranoid Survive*, he revealed his strategy on how to measure when massive changes occur, while describing how a company must adapt or fall by the wayside.

In October 2005, Grove donated $26 million to the City College of New York's School of Engineering, the largest gift ever made to the school. "Dr. Grove is the quintessential City College graduate," said President Gregory H. Williams. "He entered CCNY in 1957 as a recent immigrant, with no knowledge of English, and went on to graduate at the top of his class. He then did as much as anyone to usher in the information revolution that changed the face and pace of our world."

Andrew Grove died on March 21, 2016. By this time, he had been named TIME's Man of the Year (1997) and CEO of the Year (1997), and he had won the J.J. Ebers Award (1974) and the 1st Annual Heinz Award in Technology (1955).

Reflecting on his life, Grove observed, "I've had a wonderful life....What people are going to write about me 10 years after I'm dead—who cares?" He was wrong. Ask anyone who has a personal computer that operates because of a microprocessor chip made by Intel.

Chapter 3

GOVERNMENT AND INTERNATIONAL AFFAIRS

THE MAYORS

Abe Beame, Ed Koch and Eric Adams have three things in common. All three learned firsthand that being a big-city mayor is one of the hardest jobs there is. All three inherited very public challenges from their predecessors. And all three are CCNY alumni.

Abraham Beame

CCNY
BS, 1928

Born Abraham Birnbaum in London in 1906, Abe Beame's parents fled Warsaw, Poland, when the police sought his father for revolutionary activities against the Russian czar. When Beame was three months old, he and his mother reunited in the United States with his father, who had come to the United States first to find a home on New York's Lower East Side.

As with many immigrant children of the time, Beame started working as a child to support his family. One of his first jobs was to walk through tenement buildings to wake residents who did not own an alarm clock. In high school, he worked at a paper factory at night and studied during his dinner hour. Instead of taking the subway, he would roller skate around the city to save the cost of public transportation.

Beame attended the High School of Commerce, where he received perfect scores in the Regents bookkeeping exams. In 1928, he graduated with honors from CCNY.

After graduation, Beame opened an accounting firm, Beame and Greidinger. When the firm faltered during the Great Depression, he taught accounting at Richmond Hill High School and Rutgers University.

In 1946, Beame was named assistant budget director of New York City. By 1952, he had been promoted to budget director. During this time, he negotiated labor union contracts without strikes; tracked city revenues, expenses and debts; and implemented management policies saving the city $40 million.

Beame ran for public office for the first time in 1961. He was elected city comptroller, a position he held for four years under Democratic mayor Robert Wagner.* When Mayor Wagner retired in 1965, Beame announced his candidacy for mayor against John Lindsay, a Manhattan congressman who was nominated by both the Republican and Liberal Parties, and William F. Buckley Jr., a television personality and editor of *National Review* magazine who was the Conservative Party nominee. Reflecting on this campaign, Beame said, "I am not as ready with a quick capsule answer, but what does that have to do with being mayor? That is what I wanted to say but they [his advisors] wouldn't let me." Despite the support of Senator Robert F. Kennedy, Beame lost to the Republican nominee, John Lindsay.

For the next four years, Beame worked as an investor advisor. In 1969, the same year John Lindsay was reelected mayor, Beame ran for city comptroller again and won.

John Lindsay's two terms as mayor proved disastrous for New Yorkers. Welfare rolls doubled. New York's first personal income tax was instituted. Corporate taxes spiked. By the start of his second term, New York had lost 610,000 jobs, or 16 percent of its workforce, as corporations left New York City. All the unintended consequences of a man of good intentions—and all left for his successor to fix.

Beame won both the Democratic primary and general election in 1973, supported by Republican governor Nelson Rockefeller, who planned to run for president and needed to disassociate himself from Lindsay's failure. Beame served between 1974 and 1978, becoming the city's first Jewish mayor and the first CCNY alumni to hold the position. The goal of his

---

* Mayor Wagner created the City University of New York system, which was to become the largest urban university system in the United States. His father, U.S. Senator Robert F. Wagner, a CCNY alumni, with Al Smith authored thirty-eight new laws regulating labor in New York State in the aftermath of the Triangle Shirtwaist Factory fire.

Mayor Abe Beame on the cover of *Time* magazine, 1975.

administration was simple, as highlighted in his inaugural speech: "I want our citizens to be proud to call themselves New Yorkers."

For years as budget director and comptroller, Beame had warned of decades of unrestrained spending and accounting gimmicks used to hide

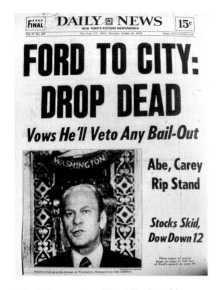

The infamous headline "Ford to City: Drop Dead" from the *Daily News* in 1975 during New York's fiscal crisis.

city deficits. The bill for all of this came due as he assumed the office of mayor.

Beame inherited the worst fiscal crisis in the city's history. The bond markets refused to issue New York City bonds when the city could not provide enough information about uncollected real estate taxes. To cover city bills, Beame cut sixty thousand city jobs, froze city wages, halted construction of police stations and firehouses, increased transit fares from thirty-five to fifty cents and imposed tuition on what had been a free city university. When Beame reached out to the federal government for help, President Gerald Ford was so unsympathetic that he inspired the headline in the *Daily News*, "Ford to City: Drop Dead."

The New York rescue plan was put together by Felix Rohatyn, a New York banker. The plan to pay off city debt came together with union pension funds, banks, the state and the federal government and the creation of the Municipal Assistance Corporation. The closest Beame came to receiving credit for saving New York City from bankruptcy was when Felix Rohatyn said, "I admire Beame for not putting the city into bankruptcy and blaming others, but for accepting the inevitable."

Beame was defeated in his bid for a second term as mayor, finishing third in the Democratic primary behind Ed Koch, who went on to become mayor, the second CCNY alumni to hold the position.

Ed Koch

CCNY
BA, 1945

"A combination of a Lindy's waiter, a Coney Island barker, a Catskill comedian, an irritated school principal and an eccentric uncle" is how Pete Hamill described Ed Koch. Ed Koch is remembered by New Yorkers of a certain age as the only mayor not afraid to shout, "How am I doin?" to anyone who would listen.

Ed Koch was born in the Bronx in 1924, the second of three children of an immigrant family from Poland. When his father's business failed during the Depression, the family moved to Newark to live with father's brother, who ran a catering business. By the time he was nine, Koch was working for his uncle in the hat and coat check concession of his uncle's Newark dance hall. While attending high school, Koch worked as a delicatessen clerk.

After Koch graduated from high school in 1941, his family moved to Brooklyn, making him eligible to attend CCNY. He worked as a shoe salesman while attending college. In 1943, Koch was drafted into the army. After being discharged in 1946, he attended NYU School of Law and practiced law in New York City for twenty years.[*]

Koch's political life began in 1952, when he became a street corner speaker for Adlai Stevenson, the democratic nominee for president. In 1956, Koch moved to Greenwich Village and joined the Village Independent Democrats as an opponent of the Tammany Hall district leader Carmine De Sapio. Koch would experience his first but not his last electoral loss in 1962 when he ran and lost the Democratic nomination for the state assembly against incumbent candidate William Passannante, the godson of De Sapio.

Undeterred, Koch ran for Greenwich Village District leader in 1963 and beat De Sapio, who had held the post for two decades. He beat De Sapio again in 1965. Koch then ran and won a seat on New York City Council, a seat he held from 1966 to 1968, when he ran for Congress. Koch held his Congressional seat for four terms, interrupted by a short-lived run for mayor in 1973, when Koch garnered little support in the primary, leading to the election of Abe Beame as mayor of New York. Koch was reelected to Congress in 1974.

In 1977, Koch won the Democratic primary election for mayor of New York against Mario Cuomo and incumbent candidate Abe Beame, who finished third. Beame's poor showing was partly the result of a massive power failure that hit the city and the "Summer of Sam,"[†] which became a symbol of big-city crime. In the general election, Koch beat Cuomo, who ran on the Liberal Party ticket. Koch would be the second Jewish mayor and the second CCNY alumni to become mayor of New York City.

---

[*] Although Koch did not return to CCNY after his service in the army, he was awarded his bachelor's degree in 1945.

[†] The "Summer of Sam" refers to the Son of Sam murders that haunted residents until the perpetrator was caught.

Mayor Ed Koch.

Koch inherited a city whose finances were dependent on the largesse of an independent agency, the Municipal Assistance Corporation. The city's credit rating was in limbo. It was not until 1982 that the city could issue bonds. City services had been cut to the bone. Times Square was a haven for pornography and prostitution, and subway trains were covered with graffiti.

In his first term as mayor, Koch held down spending, subdued municipal unions, restored the city's credit rating and revived the city's capital budget. Koch is credited with leading city government back from near bankruptcy in the 1970s to prosperity in the 1980s.

Koch's most important contribution to the city may be his housing program. Unlike his predecessor, Abe Beame, whose housing commissioner advocated planned shrinkage, a strategy whereby the city would cut losses and pull back investments and services in certain neighborhoods, Koch rebuilt devastated neighborhoods by investing billions of dollars in affordable housing for low- and middle-income New Yorkers. Eventually, more than 200,000 housing units were built or rehabilitated.

Ed Koch, who was often depicted with his arms outstretched, on the cover of TIME magazine, 1981.

Koch was reelected in 1981 with 75 percent of the vote. He became the first mayor in the city's history to get both the Democratic and Republican nominations. With a resurging economy and a $500 million surplus, city workers were rehired and municipal services restored.

Koch was reelected for a third term with 78 percent of the vote. Only two other New York City mayors in modern times, La Guardia and Robert Wagner Jr., achieved third terms. But Koch's third term would be marked by a series of scandals involving selling favors for personal gain. Although he was not implicated, Koch's reputation and his image were indelibly tarnished, and his public support diminished.

Less than two weeks after his inauguration to a third term as mayor, scandals centering on the City Transportation Department and Parking Violations Bureau exploded. Scores of convictions would be obtained by the U.S. attorney in Manhattan, Rudolph Giuliani.*

---

* As a result of recurring scandals and budget issues facing New York City, the Independent Budget Office of NYC was created in 1989. As one of more than 150 candidates, the author of this book was offered the position of (the first) director in 1990. She declined the position. Over the following years, attempts would be made to defund the office, including an attempt by Mayor Giuliani. See the appendix at the end of this book.

The first scandal, the Citisource scandal, involved Koch ally Queens Borough president Donald Manes, who committed suicide over patronage and kickback allegations involving the New York City Parking Violations Bureau. In 1986, New York City issued a contract to Citisource for handheld computers to help traffic agents issue parking tickets. Indictments would follow against a Bronx Democratic leader and five business associates on charges of fraudulently obtaining this city contract for their computer company.*

During Koch's third term, homelessness, drug-related crimes and police brutality against minorities grew. His slow response to the AIDS crisis alienated the gay community. The closing of Sydenham Hospital in Harlem based on the cost to the city and the inadequate care patients received alienated the Black community. Sydenham Hospital was one of the few hospitals that hired Black doctors in New York City.

In 1989, Koch was defeated in the primary election for mayor by David Dinkins, the Manhattan borough president. In the general election, Dinkins went on to win by a slender margin, beating Rudy Giuliani, who ran on the Republican and Liberal tickets.†

Two decades after his ignominious mayoral loss, New York City announced that it would put Koch's name on the Queensboro Bridge. The former mayor reacted saying, "There are other bridges that are more beautiful, like the GW or the Verrazano, but this more suits my personality 'cause it's a workhorse bridge." In 2022, activists attempted to undermine this belated accolade, purportedly in response to Koch's slow reaction to the AIDS crisis when he was mayor. The *New York Post* headlined, "'Woke' Democrats including AOC, Want to Strip Former Mayor Koch's Name from 59th Street (Queensboro) Bridge."

Ed Koch died in 2013. Being well aware of how fickle public opinion could be, Koch had the foresight to write his own epitaph: "He was fiercely proud of his Jewish faith, he fiercely loved the people of the city of New York and he fiercely defended the city of New York."

---

* In 1986, when she was director of finance of the City of Berkeley, the author of this book was one of the first if not the first city official to issue a contract for handheld computers for parking enforcement agents. The contract was not issued to Citisource, the scandal-ridden New York City company. Although Berkeley union officials objected to the contract as a change in job duties that was not negotiated, parking enforcement agents embraced the technology, and the city saved millions of dollars that had previously been lost because of errors in handwritten tickets.

† Perhaps the most high-profile scandal faced by the Koch administration involved Bess Myerson, Koch's commissioner of the Department of Cultural Affairs. As Myerson was a Hunter College alumna, her profile is not included in the body of this book, but it has been included at the end of this book in the appendix.

Eric Adams

CCNY (OF TECHNOLOGY)
AA, 1978

When he was sworn in as mayor in 2022, Eric Adams was the second Black mayor of New York City and the first mayor since Ed Koch to be a CCNY alumni. New Yorkers elected Adams, entering office with the longest government tenure of any mayor in seventy years, hoping that his experience would meet the challenges facing New York City. Adams's legacy is yet to be written.

Adams was born in Brooklyn in 1960, the fourth of six children. His mother worked as a housekeeper, and his father was a butcher. When he was eight years old, the family moved to South Jamaica, Queens.

When he was fourteen, Adams joined the 7-Crowns Gang. While a part of the gang, Adams and his brother were arrested for criminal trespassing, bringing him face to face with police brutality. Adams was sent to juvenile detention center and eventually put on probation. The experience would impact the rest of his life.

Adams graduated from Bayside High School in 1978. While working as a mailroom clerk and a mechanic, he received an associate degree from CCNY (of Technology) and a BA from John Jay College of Criminal Justice. Adams went on to serve for twenty-two years as an officer in the NYC Transit Police, which became part of the NYC Police Department. During that time, Adams cofounded the group Blacks in Law Enforcement Who Care, formed to prevent police brutality.

Adams's political career began and almost ended when in 1994 he ran for Congress against the incumbent in the Democratic primary. Adams did not receive enough valid signatures to make the ballot. In 1997, he registered as a Republican in protest against what he perceived as failed Democratic leadership. He changed his party registration back to Democrat in 2001.

Adams ran for a seat in the New York State Senate in 2006. He was elected and served four terms until 2013, when he was elected Brooklyn's borough president. In 2015, speaking to the graduating class at Medgar Evers College, Adams predicted that he would one day become mayor.

In 2020, Adams announced his candidacy for mayor of New York City. His campaign focused on crime and public safety. While opposed to stop-and-frisk policies during his state senate tenure, he supported the policies during the 2021 mayoral campaign. Adams won the primary and general

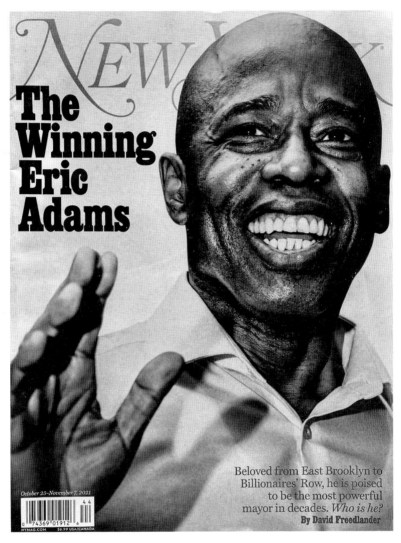

The
Winning
Eric
Adams

October 25–November 7, 2021

Beloved from East Brooklyn to
Billionaires' Row, he is poised
to be the most powerful
mayor in decades. *Who is he?*
By David Freedlander

Mayor Eric Adams, during a honeymoon period, on the cover of *New York Magazine*, 2021.

elections. He was the city's first mayor to have been elected in the Democratic primary via the ranked-choice voting system.

In his first year in office, Bill de Blasio created a universal 3-k program and began a $41 billion affordable housing program. After six years in office, he left the city in total disarray, from out-of-control crime and a demoralized police force to an unfeasible plan to replace Rikers Island. Upon taking office, Mayor Adams announced to the press, "Team de Blasio just left!"

Meeting the challenges left by his predecessor, in his first year as mayor, Adams helped pass legislation creating a public housing preservation trust, funded 1,400 new "stabilization" beds for the homeless, flooded the subway with more police and expanded child-care funding for low-income families.

Despite these achievements, rents in New York City hit historic levels, homelessness reached an all-time high and more police didn't make transit safer. In addition, Adams walked back one of his predecessor's most significant accomplishments, universal 3-k. The February 2023 Quinnipiac poll showed that Adams's job approval rating dropped to 37 percent. Despite the ratings, Adams told one friend, "I have never had so much fun in my life."

Being mayor is one of the most difficult elected offices. Adams's predecessors learned this the hard way. The job is part ambassador to NYC, to the United States and to the world, as exemplified by Ed Koch, and part 24/7 blue-collar worker and bean counter, the role assumed by Abe Beame. In his first term, Eric Adams perfected the former. His job is now to prove the latter to his constituents.

FELIX FRANKFURTER

CCNY
BA, 1902

J. Edgar Hoover referred to him as the "most dangerous man in the United States." He was a founder of the American Civil Liberties Union and a staunch supporter of judicial restraint. A man with as many friends as foes, Felix Frankfurter, associate justice of the Supreme Court, was perhaps the most controversial justice of all times.

Born in 1882 in Vienna, Austria, where his family lived in the Jewish quarter, Felix Frankfurter was the third of six children. He came to the United States with his family in 1882 when he was twelve. His family settled on the Lower East Side of New York City, a neighborhood of impoverished tenements, where his father was a door-to-door salesman. He spoke no English.

Frankfurter attended PS 25, and when not studying or playing chess, he spent hours reading at the Cooper Union for the Advancement of Science and Art and attending political lectures about trade unionism, socialism and communism. According to Frankfurter, his greatest debt to his parents was that "they left me alone almost completely."

In 1897, Frankfurter entered CCNY as part of a program that allowed him to finish high school and earn a college degree. In 1902, at nineteen, Frankfurter graduated with a high school diploma from Townsend Harris High School and with a college degree (magna cum laude) from CCNY, where he was inducted into Phi Beta Kappa.

After graduating from CCNY, Frankfurter worked for the Tenement House Department of New York City as a clerk to save money for law school. Initially, he attended New York Law School and then New York University Law School at night but found them lacking. After saving $1,200, he decided to enroll at Columbia Law School as a day student.

On his way to Morningside Heights to enroll at Columbia, Frankfurter met a City College classmate, and the two of them ended up going off to Coney Island for the day. His classmate suggested that Frankfurter go to Harvard Law School. Instead of enrolling at Columbia Law School, Frankfurter used the $1,200 he had saved to enter Harvard Law School. Frankfurter wagered that Harvard "might be as good a ticket in the lottery of chance for office as any other route."

Frankfurter graduated first in his class from Harvard Law School, where he was editor of the *Harvard Law Review*. At Harvard, Frankfurter made a network of lifelong friends, whom he would rely on in his career as a public servant, teacher of the law and judicial statesman.

In 1906, Frankfurter joined Hornblower, Byrne, Miller & Potter. This was the first time the law firm had hired a Jewish person. Within a year, Frankfurter had left private practice. Henry Stimson, the U.S. Attorney for the Southern District of New York, was looking for an assistant. Stimson asked James Barr Ames, the dean of Harvard Law School, for a recommendation. Felix Frankfurter was his choice. That same year, Frankfurter became a supporter of Theodore Roosevelt, the president of the United States and a Republican. Only three years out of law school, Frankfurter was asked by Roosevelt to comment on the president's speeches. His response to Roosevelt was, "They were fine, marred only by the number of times you employ the first person singular." There was no response from the president, who continued to use the word *I* as often if not more.

In 1911, President Taft, also a Republican, appointed Henry Stimson secretary of war. Stimson appointed Frankfurter as a law officer of the Bureau of Insular Affairs. Unhappy with the Republican Party, Frankfurter supported the Bull Moose campaign to return Theodore Roosevelt to the presidency. Disappointed when Woodrow Wilson, a Democrat, was elected, Frankfurter grew increasingly disillusioned with the established political parties, describing himself as "politically homeless."

By 1914, Frankfurter's work in Washington had impressed the faculty at Harvard Law School, leading Louis Brandeis to suggest that financier Jacob Schiff make a donation to the school to finance a position for Frankfurter. Besides teaching at Harvard, Frankfurter would help Brandeis brief and argue the constitutionality of maximum work hour and minimum wage laws before the Supreme Court. Frankfurter continued to be involved in national affairs, writing for the *New Republic* during its early years of publication.

In 1917, when the United States entered World War I, Frankfurter left Harvard to spend a weekend in Washington with his friend, Secretary of War Newton Baker. The weekend lasted two years. Frankfurter would serve as assistant to the secretaries of war and labor and finally as chairman of the War Labor Policies Board, handling wartime labor problems. He was appointed counsel to the president's Mediation Committee, established by President Wilson to resolve major strikes threatening war production. Among the disturbances he investigated were the 1916 Preparedness Day Bombing in San Francisco, where he argued that the radical leader Thomas Mooney had been entrapped.[*]

During this time, Frankfurter shared a house in the Dupont Circle neighborhood of Washington, D.C., with other bright young men, including Franklin Roosevelt, Walter Lippman, Herbert Hoover, John Foster and Allen Dulles, William Bullitt, Sumner Wells and Hamilton Fish Armstrong. The house came to be known as the House of Truth because of the philosophical discussions that took place there. The young men who lived there came to have an enormous impact on the politics of the United States in the twentieth century.

In 1919, Frankfurter was among nearly one hundred intellectuals who signed a statement of principles for the formation of the League of Nations intended to increase U.S. participation in international affairs. Encouraged by Supreme Court justice Brandeis, Frankfurter lobbied President Wilson to support the Balfour Declaration, the British government's statement in support of the establishment of a Jewish homeland in Palestine, and he served as a Zionist delegate to the Paris Peace Conference. In that year, Frankfurter also chaired a meeting in support of American recognition of the

---

[*] The same Tom Mooney memorialized by Ben Shahn in his series of paintings.

newly created Soviet Union, leading former president Theodore Roosevelt to accuse Frankfurter of being "engaged in excusing men precisely like the Bolsheviki in Russia."

At the end of World War I, with the U.S. rejection of the Treaty of Versailles and the League of Nations, Frankfurter returned to Harvard, where he remained for the next twenty years. In addition to teaching, Frankfurter continued to participate in the growing liberal movement in the United States beginning in 1918, when he attended the founding conference of the American Jewish Congress to rally for equal rights for all Americans regardless of race, religion or national ancestry. While at Harvard, Frankfurter was a founding member of the American Civil Liberties Union and served on the National Association for the Advancement of Colored People's (NAACP) National Legal Committee. When the president of Harvard proposed to limit the enrollment of Jewish students, Frankfurter worked with others to defeat the plan. It was during this time that J. Edgar Hoover began following Frankfurter, referring to him as the "most dangerous man in the United States."

In 1921, Frankfurter was awarded a chair at Harvard Law School. During this time, he authored or edited twelve books. In his speeches and writings, he remained a champion of the poor, the downtrodden, the persecuted and the wrongly convicted. In 1927, he wrote *The Case of Sacco and Vanzetti* in which he called for a new trial for anarchists Sacco and Vanzetti, asserting that their convictions were the result of anti-immigrant prejudice.[*] While his activities isolated him from his Harvard colleagues and Boston Brahmin society, Frankfurter would not be deterred, even after a Harvard alumni demanded he be fired.

Although Frankfurter was never fully accepted within government circles, he moved back to Washington, D.C., commuting to Harvard to teach. He became an advisor to President Franklin Roosevelt, a Democrat and a friend from his days living at the House of Truth. Frankfurter explained in a letter to Walter Lippman, another House of Truth alumni, that he supported FDR because of what he interpreted as Roosevelt's gradualism. Roosevelt often consulted with him about the legal implications of his New Deal legislation. Frances Perkins, the secretary of labor, admitted in her autobiography that she often asked Frankfurter for advice on drafting legislation.

During the New Deal era, Frankfurter successfully guided many bright young lawyers toward public service; they became known as Felix's Happy

---

[*] The same Sacco and Vanzetti memorialized by Ben Shahn in his series of paintings.

Hot Dogs. Among the most notable were Thomas Corcoran and Alger Hiss. Justices Oliver Wendell Holmes Jr. and Louis D. Brandeis depended on Frankfurter to appoint their law clerks, usually Frankfurter's top students. "I don't see why I am here as Postmaster General," James Farley was quoted as complaining, "since Frankfurter seems to hand out all the patronage." Frankfurter never saw it as patronage. He was helping to find able men for important government jobs. Frankfurter sent his students to Washington during both Republican and Democratic administrations.

In 1932, President Roosevelt asked Frankfurter to become part of his administration as solicitor general. Frankfurter declined. Frankfurter also turned down a nomination to the Supreme Judicial Court of Massachusetts. According to his taped interviews, published in 1960, at this time in his career Frankfurter saw himself as a professor for life. This would change following the death of Benjamin Cardozo in 1938, when FDR asked Frankfurter for recommendations of prospective candidates to fill the vacancy. Finding none on the list that suited his criteria, Roosevelt nominated Frankfurter. To quote Frankfurter, "I remember saying, and it is very natural to remember this very vividly, 'All I can say is that I wish my mother were alive.'"

Despite the fact that Frankfurter was unanimously appointed to the Supreme Court, notable opposition arose during his confirmation hearing. His nomination was violently attacked by the far right, denouncing his race, his birth (he became one of three foreign-born individuals to serve on the court) and his politics. It would be the first time in 150 years that a nominee for the Supreme Court appeared in person before the Judiciary Committee.

January 16, 1939

Newsweek

10¢

The Magazine of News Significance

Prof. Felix Frankfurter named to Supreme Court

Frankfurter served on the Supreme Court for twenty-two years from 1939 to 1962. He wrote 247 opinions for the court, 132 concurring and 251 dissents. His opinions offended both liberals and conservatives. The other associate justices either praised or scorned him. As the most outspoken advocate of judicial restraint (today he would be considered a strict constructionist), Frankfurter consistently upheld the actions of elected branches of the federal and state governments against

Opposite: Felix Frankfurter on the cover of *Newsweek* in 1939, after being appointed to the Supreme Court.

Above: Felix Frankfurter official postage stamp, 2009.

constitutional challenges so long as they did not "shock the conscience." Constitutional law professors spoke jokingly thereafter of a stomach test of constitutionality: "If it makes you sick, it's not due process."

Frankfurter's greatest contribution was not in "the particular areas of the law he illuminated, but in the conception of a judge's role that he forged." He believed that it was undemocratic for nine lifetime appointees to veto what legislators had done except in the clearest and most urgent cases." For example, in the majority opinion Frankfurter wrote in *Minersville School District v. Gobitis*, the court upheld the decision of the elected school board officials to expel the students and the constitutionality of Pennsylvania law requiring schoolchildren to salute the flag. The decision was overturned three years later.

Frankfurter helped write the Supreme Court's unanimous opinion in *Brown v. Board of Education* that declared school segregation in the United States illegal. But at the same time, he upset many liberals by refusing to protect socialists and communists blacklisted during McCarthyism. In a 5–4 decision, with Frankfurter in the majority, the court affirmed convictions of those who had refused to tell Congressional committees about alleged communist connections.

In 1948, Frankfurter hired William Thaddeus Coleman Jr., the first African American to serve as a Supreme Court law clerk. Yet in 1960, despite a recommendation from the dean of Harvard Law School, he turned down Ruth Bader Ginsburg for a clerkship position because of her gender.

In 1955, at a Harvard Law School ceremony, Frankfurter explained his often-contradictory positions: "If judges want to be preachers, they should dedicate themselves to the pulpit; if judges want to be primary shapers of policy, the Legislature is their place. Self-willed judges are the least defensible offenders against government under law."

Critics felt that Frankfurter missed greatness by taking too limited a view of the judicial function. His argumentative style was not popular among his Supreme Court colleagues. Chief Justice Earl Warren complained, "All Frankfurter does is talk, talk, talk." The contrary opinion was held by Judge Learned Hand, who wrote in 1957 that he considered Justice Frankfurter, because of his views of a judge's role, "the most important figure in our whole judicial system."

Frankfurter died in 1965 at eighty-two. No twentieth-century justice exerted more influence both positively and negatively during his tenure on the Supreme Court than Felix Frankfurter.

Benjamin Ferencz

CCNY
BSS, 1940

Benjamin Ferencz turned 101 in 2021. His tenth book was published that year. His life has been the subject of no fewer than three movies. He has received dozens of awards and accolades for his success as a human rights campaigner, including his nomination for the 2020 Nobel Peace Prize. As the last surviving prosecutor of the Nuremberg trials, he has no plans to retire. Ferencz continues to fight every day to ensure that "Law, not War" triumphs.

Benjamin Ferencz was born in 1920 on either March 11, 13 or 15—the exact date being subject to debate because there were no records kept. He described his childhood home in the Transylvania region of Hungary only

Benjamin Ferencz, *center*, chief prosecutor at the Nuremberg war crimes trial, at podium.

partly in jest as "a small house with a thatched roof, no running water, no electricity and not even a television."

Ferencz's father was trained as a shoemaker and was very proud of the fact that he could make a pair of boots out of a cow's hide. As a Jew subject to unrelenting persecution, there was no way for him to make a living in Transylvania, so he made the decision to take his wife and children to America, where he mistakenly believed that in New York there would be cows and a demand for boots. According to Ferencz, "They left for America in December, on the open deck of a so-called passenger ship. The only reason they went third class was because there was no fourth class."

When he was eighty-four, Ferencz recalled that he learned he had entered the United States under false pretenses. Since his parents spoke no English and the immigration officer at Ellis Island didn't speak Hungarian, Romanian or Yiddish, when the officer asked his parents for his name, they gave his Yiddish name, Berrel. The officer understood this as Bella and recorded Ferencz as a four-month-old girl.

The Ferencz family arrived in New York with no money, no language and nowhere to live. They spent their first weeks in America sharing a crowded space at the Hebrew Immigrant Aid Society (HIAS), an organization that provided shelter for arriving immigrants. A benevolent landlord eventually offered Ferencz's father a job as a janitor in a tenement in Hell's Kitchen. The Ferencz family could sleep in the cellar. The room where Ferencz slept had no windows. The walls were always wet due to the underground foundation, and other parts of the cellar were frequently occupied by vagrants who slept on beds of old newspapers. According to Ferencz, "It was in Hell's Kitchen that I learned about crime, that crime does not pay and with the right level of faith and commitment, you can achieve anything you want to."

When Ferencz was six, his parents divorced, and he was sent to live with an aunt in Brooklyn. He didn't start school until he was eight because he was too small, and he couldn't speak English. By the time he was thirteen, Ferencz had skipped several grades, and his teachers decided that he should go to Townsend Harris Preparatory School. If you were accepted at Townsend Harris and finished an accelerated curriculum, you were automatically accepted at the CCNY.

Ferencz graduated CCNY in 1940 with a Bachelor of Social Science degree. He knew that he wanted to attend the best law school there was but had no idea what that was. According to Ferencz, "I knew a lot of criminals but no lawyers." He wrote to one law school, Harvard, and was accepted.

As the result of his grade on his first exam in criminal law, Ferencz received a scholarship from Harvard to pay for tuition. To pay for rent, Ferencz accepted an assistantship to train other law students to write briefs. For food, he worked as a busboy at the divinity school cafeteria, where he could go in after lunch and eat enough to last for the week. When his first assistantship ended, he accepted a government grant to work as an assistant to a professor. After Roscoe Pound, a renowned jurist, rejected his application, Ferencz approached Sheldon Glueck, a leading authority in the field of juvenile crime. Juvenile crime was a subject on which Ferencz had firsthand knowledge. Glueck was writing a book on a new field, war crimes, and he needed a research analyst. Ferencz took the job so he could pay his rent. What Ferencz didn't know was that the research he was about to undertake would change his life and the practical application of international law.

When Japan attacked Pearl Harbor during his first semester at Harvard Law School, Ferencz wrote to the Federal Bureau of Investigation offering his service. He was rejected as a security risk because the FBI required that applicants be a U.S. citizen for at least fifteen years. Ferencz had been a citizen for only thirteen years. He then applied to be a pilot and was disqualified because he was too short, and he was rejected as a navigator because his eyesight was not good enough. It was not until after he completed law school and went back to his draft board that Ferencz discovered why he had not been drafted. The man in charge of his draft board had intentionally held up his draft because his own education had been sidelined after being drafted to fight in World War I. To quote Ferencz, "That of course was an indicator that unexpected, strange happenings can have a vital impact on your future life, which no one could possibly plan for and anticipate."

According to Ferencz, while he was in the army "my primary adversary was not the German army but the American army." His sergeant assigned him the dirtiest jobs possible because he was a Harvard man and a Jew. Ferencz at once applied for officer training school. When his sergeant got the papers, he tore them up and told Ferencz, "The only way you will get out of this outfit is in a box." Ferencz eventually received five battle stars from the Pentagon for surviving every major battle in Europe in World War II.

In 1944, everything changed when Ferencz received a notice that he was to report to General Patton's headquarters to establish a War Crimes branch of the Judge Advocate Section. No one knew what a war crime was. Ferencz became the first man in the U.S. Army to deal with war crimes. By this time, Ferencz was an expert on the topic, having done all the research for Professor Glueck's book when he was at Harvard. Ferencz wrote his own authorization to go anywhere and interrogate anybody. With the letter he wrote, he had the full power and authority of General Patton. According to Ferencz, "It was total improvisation," and it worked. The first war crimes trials took place in the Dachau concentration camp, on the basis of the evidence collected by Ferencz and a few coworkers.

On the day after Christmas 1945, Ferencz was honorably discharged from the U.S. Army with the rank of sergeant of infantry. He returned to New York and prepared to practice law. Ferencz was back home for a few weeks when he received a telegram from the army requesting that he return to Germany. The army offered to make him a full colonel, and he could quit anytime he wanted. Ferencz accepted the offer. He thought that he was going to Germany for a short time to have a good time. He stayed ten years.

Assigned to prosecute a broad section of Nazi criminals, Ferencz and about fifty researchers scoured Nazi offices and archives in Berlin for evidence. Everything changed when one of his staff found daily reports completed by the *Einsatzkommando*. The reports documented how many people had been killed, by which unit, who had been the officer in charge and the total killed up to that date. This was calculated, deliberate evidence of planned mass murder by the *Einsatzgruppen*, the roving extermination squads assigned to follow the Germany army as it invaded the Soviet Union in 1941 and kill communists, Romani and Jews. Ferencz requested that his assignment be changed to focus on the criminals responsible for these massacres. His immediate boss said that Ferencz could only pursue this line of inquiry if he took on the work in addition to his other work. Ferencz agreed and became chief prosecutor in the biggest murder trial in human history.

This was Ferencz's first trial. He was twenty-seven years old. He presented one witness who certified the Nazi documents that recorded the slaughter of Jews, Romani people and other civilians. He rested his case in two days. All twenty-two defendants, a group of German SS officers accused of committing the largest number of Nazi killings outside the concentration camps—more than 1 million men, women and children shot in their own towns and villages in cold blood—were convicted of war crimes and crimes against humanity.

In 1970, Ferencz decided to gradually withdraw from private practice and dedicate himself to studying, writing about and championing world peace. According to Ferencz, "Nuremberg taught me that if we did not devote ourselves to developing effective world law, the same cruel mentality that made the Holocaust possible might one day destroy the entire human race." To this end he used a set of bones from Auschwitz to persuade the German government to maintain the country's Jewish cemeteries in perpetuity. He fought for restitution for thousands of World War II victims. He argued for the creation of the International Criminal Court headquartered in The Hague that entered into force in 2002 and where he delivered the closing argument in the court's first case. He is donating his life savings to a Genocide Prevention Initiative at the Holocaust Museum.

For his work, Ferencz received a multitude of awards, including the Medal of Freedom from Harvard in 2014. The previous recipient was Nelson Mandela. In 2020, Ferencz was nominated for the Nobel Prize.

In March 2021, a bust of Ferencz was installed outside the Nuremberg courtroom where he argued almost three-quarters of a century before. Below his face is his motto, "Law, Not War."

In August 2021, his latest book, *Parting Words: Nine Lessons for a Remarkable Life*, was published. When asked what three pieces of advice he would give young people, Ferencz answered, "That's simple. One, never give up. Two, never give up. Three, never give up."*

---

* As this book was being completed, Benjamin Ferencz died at the age of 103.

HENRY KISSINGER

CCNY
ATTENDED 1941–1943

According to historian Thomas A. Schwartz, "Over the past six decades, Henry Kissinger has been America's most consistently praised and reviled public figure." At ninety-nine years old, Kissinger continues to live up to his reputation.

Henry Kissinger was born Heinz Alfred Kissinger in 1923 in Furth Bavaria near Nuremberg. Of the almost two thousand Jews in Furth before World War II, fewer than forty were left by 1945. Eleven members of the Kissinger family died at the hands of Nazis.

Kissinger's father taught in the local college preparatory school until he was fired from his job and the family lost all the rights of German citizenship. According to Thomas A. Schwartz, "The collapse of his gentle father in the face of Nazi persecution [may have] contributed to Kissinger's own sense that not only do the meek not inherit the earth, but that power is the ultimate arbiter in both life and international relations."

While Kissinger dreamed of attending the Gymnasium, a prestigious state-run high school, by the time he was old enough to apply the school had stopped accepting Jews. Instead, Kissinger attended the Israelitische Realschule, which focused on Jewish and German history, foreign languages and literature.

While his parents valued education, Kissinger preferred soccer. Because Kissinger was Jewish, he was not permitted to attend soccer matches. As Kissinger said, "All we risked was a beating." According to his cousin John, they played sports together as children. "When it was time to go in, if he [Kissinger] was ahead, we could go. But if he was losing, I'd have to keep playing until he had a chance to catch up." However improbable at the time, this competitive spirit would influence Kissinger's influence on world diplomacy during the decades to come.

In 1938, less than three months before *Kristallnacht*, the Kissinger family received permission to enter the United States by way of London. According to Kissinger, the gravity of the situation didn't hit him until visiting his grandfather for the last time. "I had never seen my father cry until he said good-bye to my mother's father. That shook me more than anything. I suddenly realized we were involved in some big and irrevocable event. It was the first time I had encountered anything my father couldn't cope with."

Reflecting on Kissinger's childhood, Fritz Kraemer, one of Kissinger's mentors, said, "Kissinger is a strong man, but the Nazis were able to damage his soul. For the formative years of his youth, he faced the horror of his world coming apart, of the father he loved being turned into a helpless mouse. It made him seek order, and it led him to hunger for acceptance, even if it meant trying to please those he considered his intellectual inferiors."

Kissinger was fifteen years old when his family arrived in America. Heinz became Henry. The Kissinger family spent the first two years in a small two-bedroom apartment in the Bronx. Kissinger's father found work as a bookkeeper, and with the help of the Council of Jewish Women, his mother built a small catering business. In 1940, the family moved to a larger apartment in Washington Heights.

After Kissinger's first year at George Washington High School, his family's uncertain finances compelled Kissinger to take a full-time job in a shaving brush factory owned by cousins of his mother. Kissinger continued to study for his diploma at night, and after completing high school, he entered CCNY. Still working during the day at the brush company, he attended CCNY at night, where he studied to be an accountant, "a nice job," Kissinger later recalled.

In 1943, at twenty years old, Kissinger was drafted into the U.S. Army. He became a U.S. citizen while completing basic training. When the engineering program he was to enter was canceled, Kissinger was reassigned. This reassignment resulted in him meeting the first of two important mentors and was the beginning of a lifetime of building a network of influential connections. Fritz Kraemer, the first of these mentors, assigned Kissinger to the Counterintelligence Corps and, more significantly, instilled in Kissinger a political philosophy based on fundamental conservatism. At the end of the war, Kissinger returned to college under the G.I. Bill. Fritz Kraemer convinced Kissinger that only Harvard was good enough for him to attend.

At Harvard, Kissinger met his second mentor, William Yandell Elliot. According to author Walter Isaacson, "At 28, he [Kissinger] was developing a power base within the academic bureaucracy. The base was the Harvard International Seminar which Elliot helped Kissinger set up. The Seminar brought aspiring young leaders to Harvard under his [Kissinger's] aegis and provided him with a network of influential acquaintances. All while he was still a graduate student, writing his dissertation and looking for larger fields to conquer."

Kissinger graduated from Harvard with a BA degree in history in 1950, an MA in 1952 and a PhD in 1954. After earning his PhD, he joined the Harvard faculty of the Department of Government, the Center for International Affairs.

When Harvard did not offer Kissinger the junior professorship he had hoped for, the dean of faculty, McGeorge Bundy, recommended him for a position at the Council on Foreign Relations in New York City, where Kissinger managed a study group on nuclear weapons. His work at the Council resulted in Kissinger's first book, *Nuclear Weapons and Foreign Policy* (1957), and his advocacy of the concept of limited nuclear war—an advocacy he would back away from in 1961 in the book *The Necessity for Choice*.

Kissinger received tenure at Harvard in 1959. Still moving between the academic and political worlds, he accepted a position as a part-time consultant in the Kennedy administration. Although a registered Democrat, Kissinger supported the presidential candidacy of Nelson Rockefeller in 1964 and 1968, attracting the attention of Richard Nixon, the man who defeated Rockefeller for the nomination in 1968.

In 1968, Henry Cabot Lodge, the ambassador to South Vietnam under Kennedy and Nixon, asked Kissinger to visit South Vietnam as a consultant. Kissinger's advice to Cabot Lodge was for the United States to negotiate its way out of the war. He did not advise Cabot Lodge how. Instead, Kissinger called for a "prayerful assessment" of the procedures and concepts that led to U.S. involvement. Nixon would appoint Kissinger to be his national security advisor.

As national security advisor, Kissinger met with North Vietnam's Le Duc Tho sixty-eight times before a ceasefire agreement known as the Paris Peace Accords was agreed on. Believing that the negotiations had been successful, Kissinger announced that "peace was at hand." For his efforts, Kissinger shared the 1973 Nobel Prize for Peace with Le Duc Tho. But the bilateral agreement had not been approved by the South Vietnamese government, and peace efforts stalled. Kissinger remained national security advisor and was named secretary of state.

Although Nixon resigned in 1974 as a result of the Watergate scandal, Kissinger continued to serve in the Ford administration, where he would advise about the need for the United States to become reengaged in Vietnam. When the capital of Vietnam, Saigon, fell to the Communist forces in 1975, Kissinger offered to return his Nobel Prize medal.

During the Nixon administration, Kissinger became a cultural icon. Dubbed the "Playboy of the Western Wing," his reputation was solidified in a 1971 article by Kandy Stroud titled "I Wonder Who's Kissing Now." Paraphrasing Napoleon, Kissinger said, "Power is the ultimate aphrodisiac."

Left: Henry Kissinger on the cover of *Time* magazine during the Nixon administration, 1973.

Right: Kissinger, while secretary of state, on the cover of *Newsweek* in 1974.

Journalists became dependent on him as their only source of information. Kissinger appeared on twenty-one covers of *Time* magazine. In 1973, Kissinger was first in a Gallup poll of the most admired Americans. According to William Buckley, "Not since Florence Nightingale has any public figure received such universal acclamation."

During the next decade, Kissinger's diplomatic efforts continued to have mixed success. He worked to ease tensions with the Soviet Union through the policy of détente, a policy he pioneered. He developed with limited success a new strategy of "triangular diplomacy," mediating between the U.S., China and the Soviet Union. He engaged in "shuttle diplomacy" between Egypt and the United States after the 1973 Yom Kippur War. He participated in the negotiations to improve East–West relations as part of the Helsinki Accord. In a less favorable light, Kissinger was involved in the electoral victory of Allende in Chile and in the defense of cutting off aid to Kurdish rebels fighting for freedom.

President Ford, in his last month in office, awarded Kissinger the Presidential Medal of Freedom (1977), the United States' highest civilian honor. In 1986, Kissinger was awarded the Medal of Liberty, which was given to ten of America's most important foreign-born leaders.

In 1978, one of Kissinger's boyhood dreams became a reality when he was named chairman of the North American Soccer League Board of Directors.

Kissinger's term as secretary of state ended in 1977. He went on to teach at Georgetown University Edmund Walsh School of Foreign Service. Following the September 11, 2001 terrorist attacks on the United States, President George W. Bush invited Kissinger to chair the commission of inquiry into the attacks. In 1982, Kissinger founded the consulting firm Kissinger and Associates.

At ninety-nine years old, Kissinger continues to serve as chairman of his consulting firm, and he wrote his nineteenth book, *Leadership: Six Studies in World Strategy*. In November 2022, he was hired by Deutsche Bank to a new advisory board. He continues to be involved in international affairs, publicly arguing that Ukraine should cede portions of its internationally recognized territory seized by Russia.

Kissinger continues to live up to Thomas A. Schwartz's depiction as one of America's most consistently praised and reviled public figures.

COLIN POWELL

CCNY
BS, 1958

Commenting on Colin Powell's long career, President George W. Bush said, "Colin Powell was so respected that he was given the Presidential Medal of Freedom twice." Powell achieved this distinction by serving his country in the military for forty years, earning the rank of four-star general and serving his government as national security advisor, chairman of the Joint Chiefs of Staff and secretary of state—all with distinction but not without controversy.

Born in Harlem in 1937 as the son of Jamaican immigrants, Powell was raised in the South Bronx by his father, a shipping clerk, and his mother, a seamstress.

Describing the neighborhood of his youth, Powell wrote in his 1995 autobiography, *My American Journey*, "There was no majority [in my neighborhood]. Everybody was either a Jew, an Italian, a Pole, a Greek, a Puerto Rican or as we said in those days, a Negro."

While attending New York City public schools, Powell served as a Shabbos goy, helping Orthodox Jewish families with tasks on the Sabbath and working at a local baby furniture store, where he learned Yiddish from the eastern European Jewish shopkeepers. In his book *It Worked for Me*, Powell wrote about how in his youth he did not live up to his parents' expectations. "My cousins became lawyers and doctors and judges, and I just sort of hung around." According to Powell, it was the store owner where he worked who helped change his life by insisting that he had more potential and should get an education.

In 1954, Powell, a straight C student from the South Bronx, enrolled in CCNY as a geology major. According to Powell, "I typified the students that CCNY was created to serve, the sons and daughters of the inner city, the poor, the immigrant. Many of my classmates had the brainpower to attend Harvard, Yale, or Princeton. What they lacked was money and influential connections. Yet they went on to compete with and surpass alumni of the most prestigious private campuses in this country."

While it was the circumstances of his birth that brought Powell to CCNY, it was ROTC that kept him enrolled, helped him improve his GPA and changed his life. According to Powell, "I got straight A's in ROTC, so the administration rolled my A's into the overall grade point average and that got me to a 2.0."

Commenting on his life and his career in an interview with NPR's Robert Siegel, Powell remarked, "People have asked me, 'What would you have done if you hadn't gone into the Army?' I say I'd probably be a bus driver, I don't know."

Describing his experience in ROTC as one of the happiest experiences in his life, Powell said, "It was only once I was in college, about six months into college when I found something I liked, and that was ROTC, Reserved Officer Training Corps. And not only did I like it, but I was pretty good at it. That's what you really have to look for in life, something that you like, and something that you think you're pretty good at. And if you can put those two things together, then you're on the right track, and just drive on....I found my place. I found discipline. I found structure. I found people that were like me, and I liked, and I fell in love with the Army those first few months in ROTC, and it lasted for the next forty odd years."

In 1958, Powell graduated from CCNY with a Bachelor of Science degree in geology and a commission as army second lieutenant. After completing two tours in Vietnam (1962–63 as a major and 1968 as assistant chief of staff of operations for the 23rd Infantry Division), Powell returned to the United States in 1971 with the Soldier's Medal for Bravery.

After earning an MBA from George Washington University, Powell would serve five presidents (Nixon, Reagan, George H.W. Bush, Bill Clinton and George W. Bush) over the next three decades.

From 1971 to 1973, Powell served as a White House Fellow under President Richard Nixon, and from 1987 to 1989, he served as national security advisor under President Ronald Reagan, playing a key role in cementing the historic relationship between Reagan and Mikhail Gorbachev.

Powell's last military assignment was in 1989, when George H.W. Bush selected him as chairman of the Joint Chiefs of Staff, the highest military position in the Department of Defense. During his time as chairman, Powell oversaw twenty-eight crises and formulated the Powell Doctrine, which limits American military action unless it satisfies criteria regarding American national security interest, overwhelming force and widespread public support. This approach, designed to "maximize the potential for success while minimizing casualties," was successfully applied to Operation Desert Storm in 1991. With a promotion to four-star general by Bush, Powell became the third general since World War II to reach four-star rank without serving as a division commander. The other two generals were Dwight Eisenhower and Alexander Haig.

Although Powell resigned his military position as chairman of the Joint Chiefs of Staff in 1993, ten years later, he would find himself embroiled in a military controversy that would shadow the rest of his life.

The controversy had its inception in 2001, when in the lead-up to the 2003 invasion of Iraq, George W. Bush named Powell secretary of state. Opposed to the forcible overthrow of Saddam Hussein, Powell eventually agreed to go along with the Bush administration's plan to remove Saddam as long as there was support from the international community. To garner that support, Powell spoke before the U.N. Security Council, arguing that Saddam had an arsenal of weapons of mass destruction. But the facts did not support Powell's claim. Saddam had no weapons of mass destruction. According to Powell, "When I presented it to the U.N. I had every assurance from the intelligence community that the information I had was correct. It turned out not to be." In a 2005 interview with Barbara Walters, Powell acknowledged, "It was a blot on my record.…It became a source of lifelong regret."

In 2004, Powell announced that he would resign as secretary of state after President Bush was reelected. The following day, Bush nominated National Security Advisor Condoleezza Rice as Powell's successor, although Powell had announced that he would stay on until the end of Bush's first term.

Powell memorialized his military legacy in the "13 Rules of Leadership," published in *It Worked for Me*. Following his own advice—"Avoid having your ego so close to your position that when your position fails, your ego goes with it"—Powell entered his post-military career with his ego bruised but not beaten.

Identified as a lifelong Independent while in uniform, Powell declared himself a Republican from 1995 until 2021. In 2021, he again became an Independent following the violence at the U.S. Capitol. After serving presidents of both parties, Powell was pursued by both Democrats and Republicans for his endorsement, which he gave cautiously, endorsing (with qualifications) Barack Obama, Hillary Clinton and Joe Biden.

In 1996, Powell was mentioned as a Republican presidential candidate to run against Bill Clinton. The closest he got to running for president was winning the Republican New Hampshire presidential primary on write-in votes. Deciding not to run, Powell commented, "In one generation, we have moved from denying a Black man service at a lunch counter, to elevating one to the highest military office in the nation, and to being a serious contender for the presidency. This is a magnificent country, and I am proud to be one of its sons."

In 2000, Powell endorsed George W. Bush, under whose father Powell had served as chairman of the Joint Chiefs of Staff a decade earlier. Bush won and appointed Powell secretary of state. At Powell's swearing-in ceremony, Bush, giving a nod to the Powell Doctrine formulated during his father's administration, described Powell: "He is a leader who understands America must work closely with our friends in times of calm if we want to be able to call on them in times of crisis."

In 2008, with two weeks left in the presidential campaign, Powell, a Republican, endorsed Barack Obama. Although there was talk that Powell might be offered a cabinet position, the offer did not materialize. In the end, Powell became a critic of the Obama administration because of Obama's unfulfilled promise to close Guantanamo and Obama's failure to implement policies to promote a faster economic recovery.

Colin Powell, often rumored as a potential presidential candidate throughout his career, on the cover of *TIME* magazine in 1995.

In 2013, CCNY's School of Social Sciences was renamed the Colin Powell School for Civic and Global Leadership. Recalling Powell's dedication to CCNY and the opportunities the school opened for him, Marc Benioff of *Time* magazine noted, "Colin Powell knew that one of the best antidotes to inequality is education and that business has a responsibility to help."

Condoleezza Rice, former secretary of state, wrote, "He found great fulfillment in the creation of the Colin Powell School for Civic and Global Leadership at the City College of New York. The school would, he hoped, make possible more stories like his: a son of immigrants who, as he freely admitted, wandered for a while until the military gave him a sense of purpose and discipline."

Colin Powell official postage stamp from Tanzania.

A banner in the sixth-floor atrium of CCNY's North Academic Center, home of the Colin Powell School, lays out Powell's 13 Rules of Leadership.

Controversy followed Powell again in 2016 when presidential candidate Hillary Clinton attempted to enmesh him into the scandal related to her use of a private mail server when she was secretary of state. Commenting on Clinton, the e-mail scandal and the 2012 Benghazi attack controversy, Powell said, "Everything [Clinton] touches she kind of screws up." As with his endorsement of Obama, a few weeks before the 2016 election, Powell nonetheless endorsed Clinton, stating, "Because I think she is qualified, and the other gentleman [Trump] is not qualified."

Colin Powell died on October 18, 2021, at eighty-four as this profile was being written. Of all the eulogies at his funeral, none mentioned Powell's speech to the United Nations in 2003 or the controversy that followed. Michael Powell, Colin Powell's son, summed up his father's life: "The example of Colin Powell does not call on us to emulate his résumé; it is to emulate his character and his example as a human being."

Chapter 4

LITERATURE AND SCREENWRITING

UPTON SINCLAIR

CCNY
HS, 1897

Upton Sinclair was born in Baltimore, Maryland, in 1878. His father was a liquor salesman whose heavy drinking cast a shadow over Sinclair's childhood. His mother was a teetotaler. Sinclair described his childhood as a series of "Cinderella transformations"—one day he would be staying in the lavish home of his maternal grandparents and the next his family would be living in a boardinghouse and Sinclair would be sharing a bed with his mother. Sinclair's worldview was shaped by this irreconcilable dichotomy. It was this backdrop that produced one of America's premier investigative journalists.

Because of his family's frequent moves, Sinclair did not start school until he was ten years old. As an escape from his dysfunctional home life, at five years old Sinclair turned to reading to expand his universe.

In 1892, at fourteen years old, Sinclair entered CCNY, at that time a high school. To earn extra income, he wrote dime novels, jokes and articles for pulp magazines. At seventeen, with this extra money, Sinclair moved his family into a better apartment.

Sinclair graduated from CCNY High School in 1897 and enrolled in Columbia University. He planned to study law but was drawn to literature. At Columbia, he paid the one-time enrollment fee to learn a variety of subjects, signing up for a class and then later dropping it. In 1902, he joined the Socialist Party. Later, he would form the Intercollegiate Socialist Society with future novelist Jack London. Sinclair continued to support himself by writing pulp fiction and boys' short stories.

Between 1901 and 1906, after leaving Columbia, Sinclair wrote four novels: *King Midas* (1901), *Prince Hagen* (1903), *The Journal of Arthur Stirling* (1903) and *Manassas* (1904). Although the novels enjoyed critical success, few copies were sold. Then Sinclair found opportunity in the bowels of Chicago's meatpacking district.

In 1904, the editors of the socialist newspaper *Appeal to Reason* gave Sinclair a $500 advance and sent him to Packingtown, where he spent seven weeks in disguise observing the lives and working conditions of stockyard workers in Chicago's meatpacking district. "I talked, not merely with the working men and their families, but with bosses and superintendents," said Sinclair, "with night-watchmen and saloon-keepers and policemen, with doctors and lawyers and merchants, with politicians and clergymen and settlement workers." He witnessed contaminated and diseased carcasses, rat infestations and severed human appendages mixing with meats. From his observations, Sinclair wrote the groundbreaking exposé *The Jungle*.

The Jungle was first published serially in *Appeal to Reason*. Thought too controversial by many publishers, it was published as a single novel only after Sinclair financed the publication himself. In 1906, the mainstream publisher Doubleday, Page & Company, anticipating a bestseller, agreed to publish *The Jungle*. It was a success, being translated into seventeen languages within months of publication.

Written as fiction, according to Sinclair the story was "intended to set forth the breaking of human hearts by a system which exploits the labor of men and women for profit." Fiction became fact, and as the result of a review by Jack London, *The Jungle* became known as the "*Uncle Tom's Cabin* of wage slavery."

After publication, the public outcry was so loud that it reached the ears of President Theodore Roosevelt. Roosevelt was slow to react until he read *The Jungle* for himself. The president was so appalled that he reportedly threw sausage he was eating out of the window and then invited Sinclair to the White House.

In 1906, after an official investigation confirmed the conditions described in *The Jungle*, the Meat Inspection Act and the Pure Food and Drug Act were signed into law, mandating that all livestock be inspected before being slaughtered and processed for human consumption and prohibiting "the manufacture, sale, or transportation of adulterated or misbranded or poisonous or deleterious foods, drugs or medicines, and liquors."

Since its publication, *The Jungle* has never been out of print. But despite its success, Sinclair was disappointed in the public's reaction. As an avowed socialist, his objective in writing *The Jungle* was to highlight the dehumanization of wage workers and stop the brutal mistreatment of animals. But the public cared only that they were consuming tainted meat. To quote Sinclair, "I aimed at the public's heart and by accident I hit it in the stomach."

Disillusioned when *The Jungle* did not advance his socialist agenda, Sinclair used $30,000 earned from book sales to create an experimental cooperative community called Helicon Home Colony. Located in

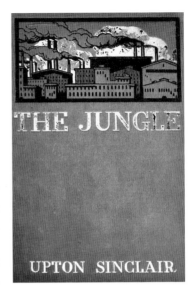

Upton Sinclair's most famous book, *The Jungle*.

Englewood, New Jersey, Helicon Home was what Sinclair considered to be the future of American living, where members could escape the menial work of domestic life. He sought "authors, artists, musicians, editors, teachers and professional men" who wanted to "avoid the drudgeries of domestic life" to live there. The colony had a rigorous screening process for applicants, including a restriction against those of color, explicitly banning Black people and less publicly banning Jews. During its existence, about forty-six adults and fifteen children lived there. The colony lasted six months before it was destroyed by a fire in 1907.

Sinclair spent the next few years as a nomad, moving throughout Europe and the United States until he settled in California in the 1920s, where he founded the state's chapter of the American Civil Liberties Union.* He unsuccessfully ran twice for the U.S. Congress on the Socialist Party ticket and was the Socialist Party candidate for governor of California in 1926 and 1930. In 1934, Sinclair ran for governor of California as a Democrat. His platform, known as the End Poverty in California movement (EPIC), electrified the Democratic Party, and Sinclair gained the Democratic nomination. Incumbent governor Frank Merriam defeated Sinclair by a sizable margin in the general election.

---

* The ACLU was co-founded by CCNY alumni Felix Frankfurter in 1920.

Unsuccessful in politics and facing negative advertising financed by movie industry executives, Sinclair returned to writing. Of the more than eighty books Sinclair wrote, his most successful were focused on social research. As critic Alfred Kazin stated, Upton Sinclair was "one of the great social historians of the modern era." His works include *King Coal* (1917), *The Profits of Religion* (1917), *The Goose-Step* (1923), *Oil!* (1927) and *The Flivver King* (1937). In 1928, he wrote the popular book *Boston*, inspired by the Sacco-Vanzetti trial, and in 1943 he won the Pulitzer Prize for his book *Dragon's Teeth*, which explored the Nazi occupation of Germany.

Although none of Sinclair's subsequent books matched the success of *The Jungle*, *The Brass Check* (1919), like *The Jungle*, was an incriminating critique of an industry, this time journalism. *The Brass Check* exposed slanted news sources that only printed stories that benefited the men who owned the newspapers. Sinclair called the work "the most important and most dangerous book I have ever written." Most magazines and newspapers, including the *New York Times*, refused to run paid advertisements or review the book for fear of providing unintentional advertising. Despite this, there were ten printings of *The Brass Check* in its first decade, and it sold more than 150,000 copies. Four years after the publication of *The Brass Check*, the journalists code of ethics was created.

Although personal and professional disappointment plagued Sinclair throughout his life, the impact of his work on the lives of every American is undeniable. While Sinclair's goal of addressing the dehumanization of wage workers would have to wait until the rise of labor unions in the United States, the creation of the Food and Drug Administration (FDA) is a direct result of the public outcry after the publication of *The Jungle*. Created to protect the public health of all Americans by ensuring the safety of our nation's food supply, cosmetics and products that emit radiation as well as the safety, efficacy and security of human and veterinary drugs, biological products and medical devices, the FDA is Sinclair's legacy to future generations of all Americans.

After a lifetime advocating for the underdog, Upton Sinclair died in 1968. He was ninety years old.

Upton Sinclair on the cover of *Time* magazine, 1934.

Paddy Chayefsky

CCNY
BA, 1943

"I'm mad as hell, and I'm not going to take this anymore," one of the most recognizable lines in movie history, was written by Paddy Chayefsky, a Bronx native and son of Russian immigrants. Like Howard Beale, who memorialized the iconic line in the movie *Network*, Chayefsky's life and his work were the product of personal and professional frustrations and awards.

Born Sidney Aaron Chayefsky in 1923, Chayefsky was a conversational speaker at two and a half and at age twelve entered De Witt Clinton High School, where he was a contributor to and the editor of the *Magpie*, the school newspaper. Marcella Whalen, the literary advisor of the *Magpie* at the time, forecasting things to come, noted that Chayefsky's submissions "needed no editing or proofreading. There were never even typing or spelling errors."

In 1939, at the age of sixteen, Chayefsky, an "A student," graduated from high school, listing "Muckracking" as his ambition in his high school yearbook. Chayefsky knew that the road he would follow was not going to be without controversy.

Although Chayefsky entered CCNY with the ambition to be a writer, he graduated in 1943 with a BA in accounting and social sciences. Two weeks before graduation, he was drafted into the U.S. Army.

Chayefsky could not foresee the lasting impact the army would have on his identity. As he had never been away from home before, adopting to army life was a challenge. To avoid 5:00 a.m. kitchen duty, Chayefsky, who was Jewish, asked to be excused to attend Mass. In response to his commanding officer questioning his religious affiliation, Chayefsky replied that his father was Jewish and his mother was Irish. The officer responded, "OK Paddy," and the name stuck.

While serving with the 104th Infantry Division in Germany, Chayefsky was wounded by a land mine, earning him a Purple Heart and disfiguring him for life. The disfigurement, compounded by an early rejection by a girl, reinforced a shyness around women that would follow him throughout his personal life and influence much of his professional work.

While recovering from his army injuries in a hospital in England, Chayefsky wrote a GI musical comedy called *No T.O. for Love*. The show was produced by the Special Services Unit in 1945 and toured European army bases for

Paddy Chayefsky around the time he wrote *Network* for United Artists.

two years. This initial success as a playwright was fleeting for Chayefsky. It would be years before his name would again appear on a playbill.

Upon returning to the United States, Chayefsky worked in his uncle's print shop while writing dramas and short stories for TV and radio programs. During this time, he wrote a second play, *Put Them All Together*. It was never produced. Chayefsky then authored a short story, "The Great American Hoax," and sold it to *Good Housekeeping* magazine. It was never published.

In 1947, Chayefsky left New York for Hollywood and the promise of success as a screenwriter. He landed a job at Universal Pictures in the accounting department. Frustrated, he returned to New York City and was hired as an apprentice scriptwriter but was fired after six weeks. In 1948, he returned to Hollywood after the movie rights were sold for a novella he wrote. Frustrated again by rewrites that were demanded of him, Chayefsky quit and moved back to New York City to write adaptations for radio.

Although Chayefsky, an opponent of McCarthy and HUAC, appeared in the anti-communist publication *Firing Line*, he was not called before the committee nor was he blacklisted. In later years, he would vocally oppose the Vietnam War and support the cause of Soviet Jewry.

Chayefsky's professional luck changed with the dawn of the Golden Age of Television, the era when TV sets were expensive, viewers were wealthy and dramas were in vogue. His first script telecast in 1949 was an adaptation of Budd Schulberg's *What Makes Sammy Run?*, a play that chronicles the rise and fall of Sammy Glick, who climbs to the top of the movie business by deception and betrayal. Chayefsky achieved his high school ambition and had become a muckraker.

Success followed Chayefsky when in 1953, during rehearsals of *The Reluctant Citizen* in the Old Abbey Hotel in New York City, he spotted a sign that read, "Girls, Dance with the Man Who Asks You. Remember, Men Have Feelings, Too." This prompted him to begin writing *Love Story* about a young woman. During the process of developing the story, the drama changed focus and became a story about "a guy who goes to a ballroom." According to Chayefsky, "I didn't want my hero to be handsome, and I didn't want the girl to be pretty. I wanted to write a love story the way it would literally have happened to the kind of people I

Advertisement for the award-winning film *Network*, written by Paddy Chayefsky, directed by Sidney Lumet and starring Faye Dunaway, William Holden, Peter Finch and Robert Duvall.

know." When the lead character described himself as "a fat little ugly guy and girls don't go for me, that's all," Chayefsky was describing himself and the personal rejections he had experienced as a young man.

The title *Love Story* was unacceptable to NBC, so Chayefsky used his alternative title, *Marty*. *Marty* premiered on *Philco Television Playhouse* in 1953. A decade later, *Marty* would be selected for showing at the Museum of Modern Art "as part of a retrospective of the best that had been done in American television," according to curator Richard Griffith.

Harold Hecht bought the film rights for *Marty*, thinking it would be a flop and that *Marty* would be a tax loss to offset successes he had earlier in the year. Chayefsky was initially uninterested in the project, remembering the frustration of working in Hollywood years before. When Hecht agreed to give him creative control, Chayefsky accepted. This would be the first Hollywood film to be populated solely by average-looking characters.

After studio production stoppages due to accounting and financial difficulties, the low-budget independently produced film *Marty* won four Academy Awards (Best Picture, Best Director, Best Screenplay and Best Actor). Hecht's Academy Award acceptance speech began, "It's very fortunate to live in a country where any man, no matter how humble his origin, can become president, and to be part of an industry where any picture, no matter how low its budget, can win the Oscar."

For the next ten years, Chayefsky found moderate Broadway theatrical success coupled with box office failure. In 1960, his play *The Tenth Man* won Tony Award nominations for Best Play, Best Director and Best Scenic Design. In 1964, *The Americanization of Emily* was a box office failure as a result of its antiwar stance. This was followed by Chayefsky's firing as the screenwriter for *The Cincinnati Kid* and the screen adaptation of the musical *Paint Your Wagon*.

By 1971, Chayefsky's professional fortunes had changed when he won his second Academy Award for *The Hospital*, a screenplay he wrote after his wife received poor care at a hospital. Again, he negotiated to retain creative control, and the leading character would embody many of Chayefsky's personal traits.

In 1976, Chayefsky won his third Academy Award for *Network*, the story of how TV news had abandoned quality reporting for sensationalism in the pursuit of high ratings and profits. *Network* centers on the frustrations (not dissimilar to Chayefsky's) of an evening newscaster unable to survive in the television industry. The film was a commercial success and won four Academy Awards, for Best Actor, Best Actress, Best Supporting Actress and

Best Original Screenplay. In 2000, the film was selected for preservation in the U.S. National Film Registry by the Library of Congress as being "culturally, historically, or aesthetically significant." In 20002, *Network* was inducted into the Producers Guild of America Hall of Fame as a film that has "set an enduring standard for American entertainment." In 2005, the two Writers Guilds of America voted Chayefsky's script one of the ten greatest screenplays in the history of cinema.

During one of his last interviews, Chayefsky lamented, "A writer is what he writes, and I would like to be remembered as a good writer. I would like the stuff I write to be done and read for many generations. I just hope the world lasts that long."

Chayefsky's last project was a political play about the Alger Hiss trial.* Chayefsky died at fifty-eight years of age in 1981 before the play was completed.

Fulfilling a promise made to Chayefsky, Bob Fosse tap-danced at his funeral. Three years after his death, Chayefsky was part of the inaugural class of inductees into the Academy of Television Arts & Sciences Television Hall of Fame.

Aaron Sorkin, who cited Chayefsky when he accepted his Oscar for the screenplay *The Social Network*, wrote in an e-mail, "No predictor of the future—not even Orwell—has ever been as right as Chayefsky was when he wrote *Network*."

Mario Puzo

CCNY
Attended 1949

Mario Puzo was a made man, but not in the customary sense. Puzo created one of the most popular mobster novels ever written, *The Godfather*. It would make the life of the wise guy part of mainstream vernacular.

Puzo was born in 1920 in Hell's Kitchen to illiterate Italian immigrants. He grew up in an overcrowded tenement building with his parents and

---

* Alger Hiss was a top law school student of Felix Frankfurter, another CCNY alumni profiled in this book. Frankfurter recommended Hiss as an aide to President Franklin Roosevelt. During his time in the Roosevelt administration, Hiss was accused by Richard Nixon of being a communist spy after classified papers were found in a "pumpkin patch" on Hiss's estate. Hiss was convicted, and Nixon's political career advanced.

six siblings. His father was a railroad trackman for the New York Central Railroad who worked fourteen-hour days with little pay. When Puzo was twelve, his father was diagnosed with schizophrenia and hospitalized. His father's absence was no loss to his mother.

Left to raise her seven children alone, according to Puzo his mother "would rather live on welfare than have his father return home....My father was committed to an insane asylum and when he could have returned home, my mother made the decision not to let him out. He would have been a burden on the family. That's a Mafia decision."

Mafia decisions were not uncommon for Puzo's mother. A ruthless person when it came to defending, protecting and disciplining her children, she would inspire one of the most famous Mafia characters, Don Vito Corleone from *The Godfather*. According to Puzo, "Whenever the Godfather opened his mouth, in my own mind I heard the voice of my mother. I heard her wisdom, her ruthlessness, and her unconquerable love for her family and for life itself....The Don's courage and loyalty came from her; his humanity came from her." Through his mother, Puzo transformed a matriarch into a mobster, and *The Godfather* was born. But not before Puzo paid his dues.

Thanks to his mother, Puzo found safety at home. He found a space to play sports, socialize and learn about the library at the Hudson Guild, a community organization founded in 1897 to help the working class improve living conditions. The Hudson Guild also offered Puzo the opportunity to participate in the Fresh Air Fund's program for poor city youth. Between 1929 and 1935, Puzo spent two weeks of the summer with a family in New Hampshire. Unfortunately, this escape was only temporary. According to Puzo, "From this Paradise I was flung into Hell....I had to help support my family by working on the railroad."

While Puzo spent his teen years as a switchboard worker for the New York Central Railroad, the 11th Avenue Public Library became his haven away from home and work. Distracted by writers like Dostoyevsky, Puzo more than once neglected his switchboard post, bringing all trains to a screeching halt. Working on the railroad would not be Puzo's permanent career.

With Puzo's love for reading came a talent for writing that brought him to the attention of his English teacher at Commerce High School. But before his talent could be realized, World War II began and Puzo was drafted.

Puzo's time in military service was not without its problems. A self-proclaimed wimp and inept soldier with bad eyesight, Puzo saw little action.

Although he rarely held a gun, after coming under fire in France, he won five battlefield stars.

In 1949, Puzo returned to the United States with his wife, whom he met while he was in the service, and a young family to support. Like many returning soldiers, he resumed his education under the G.I. Bill, attending writing courses at CCNY, Columbia University and the New School for Social Research.

At thirty, Puzo published his first short story, "The Last Christmas," in *American Vanguard*, a publication that prioritized the work of postwar authors. Although critically successful, "The Last Christmas" did little to launch Puzo's writing career. In order to support his growing family, Puzo took a job as a low-level government clerk. He continued writing at night.

For the next few years, Puzo worked two jobs to support his family while submitting short stories to literary journals and magazines. Most were rejected until, in 1954, Random House picked up his first novel, *The Dark Arena*. Published in 1955, Puzo's debut novel received positive reviews, but the book did not sell.

Fate intervened when Puzo suffered a severe gallbladder attack. While exiting a taxi taking him to the Veterans Administration Hospital for treatment, Puzo fell into the gutter and had an epiphany: "There I was lying there thinking, here I am, a published writer, and I am dying like a dog. That's when I decided I would be rich and famous." Puzo set out to write the next bestseller.

Puzo's second novel took inspiration from life. *The Fortunate Pilgrim* (1964) told the story of Italian immigrants in Depression-era New York City. According to critics, this book "could have put Puzo on track to be the Italian Malamud or Henry Roth." Again, despite earning critical acclaim, his novel did not sell.

By age forty-five, Puzo's first two novels had earned him a combined sum of $6,500. By this time, he had accumulated a considerable amount of debt. To quote his son Tony, "[Puzo] liked to do things first-class even though we only had fifth-class money." Faced with economic reality, Puzo wrote a ten-page outline about Italian Americans in organized crime titled *The Godfather*. After pitching the idea to G.P. Putnam's Sons, the publisher gave him "an offer he couldn't refuse": the publication of his book and a $5,000 advance. In 1968, upon finishing *The Godfather*, true to form Puzo used the final installment of his advance to take his family on a trip to Europe. Little did he know how his life was to change upon his return.

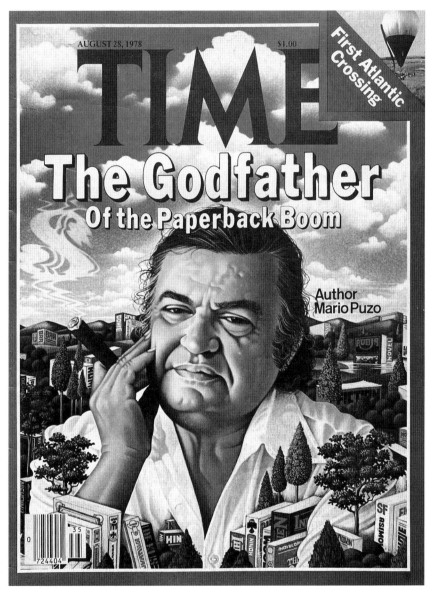

Author Mario Puzo, whose *Godfather* series is one of the best-selling books of all time, on the cover of *TIME* magazine in 1978.

Before *The Godfather* was released as a hardback, the book's paperback rights sold for $410,000, breaking previous sale records by $10,000. Upon publication, *The Godfather* became a worldwide phenomenon. It landed on the U.S. bestsellers list and kept its place for sixty-seven weeks.

Mario Puzo official postage stamp from Togo, 2019.

The success of *The Godfather* was boosted by the 1972 movie adaptation, directed and cowritten by Francis Ford Coppola and starring Marlon Brando, Al Pacino and James Caan. Although Al Ruddy, the film's producer, was apprehensive about bringing Puzo on as a screenwriter, Puzo was determined to be involved in the adaptation of his book to the screen. According to Ruddy, "Mario said, 'If you hire me, I promise you I will never look at this book again.' And he threw his copy of the book on the floor at the restaurant. I gave him the job." Puzo became a screenwriter.

Although the film was widely successful, redefining the gangster genre by humanizing mobsters and blurring the lines between hero and villain, Puzo's story did not receive universal rave reviews. Some Italian Americans saw the story as promoting negative stereotypes. The most surprising responses to *The Godfather* came from mobsters themselves. After the release of the movie *The Godfather*, Puzo was approached by two Mafia members, including

Chicago mobster John Rosselli, who insisted that Puzo must have talked to the "top guys" in order to write the story. To these claims, Puzo replied, "'I'm ashamed to admit that I wrote *The Godfather* entirely from research. I never met a real honest-to-G-d gangster. I knew the gambling world pretty good, but that's all."

A second *Godfather* movie was released in 1974 and a third in 1990. Puzo received Academy Awards for Best Screenplay for the first two movies. Owing to its success, *The Godfather* franchise led to a series of Mafia-inspired shows and stories, including the TV series *The Sopranos*. Puzo was a screenwriter for *Earthquake*, *Superman*, *Superman II* and *The Cotton Club*. During this time, he also wrote four novels: *Fools Die* (1978), *The Sicilian* (1984), *The Fourth K.* (1991) and *The Last Don* (1996).

Mario Puzo died of heart failure in 1999. His last books, *Omerta* (2000) and *The Family* (2002), were published posthumously. Until his death, Puzo thought of himself as "a working-class novelist." According to the author of *The Godfather*, "I am another Italian success story. Not as great as DiMaggio or Sinatra but quite enough."

Chapter 5

MUSIC

IRA GERSHWIN

CCNY
ATTENDED 1914–1916

Ira Gershwin, the first lyricist to be awarded a Pulitzer Prize, was born Israel Gershowitz in 1896, the oldest of four children of Russian immigrants.

Gershwin's grandfather was born in Odessa and served for twenty-five years as a mechanic for the Imperial Russian Army to earn the right of free travel and residence as a Jew. His son Moishe worked as a leather cutter of women's shoes. Faced with compulsory military service if he remained in Russia, Moishe immigrated in 1891 to New York, where he changed his name to Morris Gershwine, married and began a family.

Morris Gershwine undertook a variety of jobs, including the designer of uppers for women's shoes and a proprietor of a cigar store, a billiard parlor and a restaurant. The family (including children Ira, George, Arthur and Francis), always residing where Morris worked, lived in twenty-eight homes in Manhattan and Brooklyn. In addition to changing jobs and homes, Morris changed the family last name to Gershvin, finally settling on Gershwin after their second son, George, changed his last name. Ira Gershwin, known as "Izzy" as a child, believed that his name was Isidore until he applied for a passport and learned his given name.

Ira Gershwin.

When Ira was ten years old, his parents bought him a piano. Ira and his brother George, then eight years old, took piano lessons from an aunt. To his parents' surprise and Ira's relief, it was his brother George who took an interest in playing. Ira preferred reading nickel novels and writing.

Gershwin attended Townsend Harris High School. He managed to fail in subjects like French, geometry and analytical drawing but always was active in the school newspaper. It was at Townsend Harris that Gershwin met Yip Harburg, another CCNY alumni, and the two became lifelong friends, bonding over a love of Gilbert and Sullivan.

Between 1914 and 1916, Gershwin attended CCNY. As a sophomore, he was still taking first-year math classes, and at the prospect of taking calculus in the future, Gershwin dropped out of CCNY to pursue a writing career.

After dropping out of college, Gershwin, like his father, worked in a series of odd jobs, including steam room attendant, carnival helper and photographer's assistant. Occasionally, he would write theater reviews but did not show promise as a writer until 1917, when his short story "The Shrine" appeared in *Smart Set*, an H.L. Mencken publication. The work was published under the pseudonym "Bruskin Gershwin." He received a check for one dollar and immediately spent it on postage to submit additional articles. The submissions were all rejected.

In 1918, while Gershwin was working as a desk attendant in a Turkish bath, his brother George asked him to write a set of lyrics for a song he was writing. "The Real American Folk Song" was the earliest published collaboration of George and Ira Gershwin. Ira used the pseudonym "Arthur Francis," the first names of his youngest brother and sister, to eliminate confusion with his younger brother George. As Arthur Francis, Gershwin also wrote the lyrics to his first full Broadway show, *Two Little Girls in Blue* (1921), and *I'll Build a Stairway to Paradise* (1922). To protect his brother Ira's privacy, when anyone asked to see Arthur Francis, George would respond, "Mr. Francis is too busy to be disturbed."

Gershwin continued to shun the limelight: "I always felt that if George hadn't been my brother and pushed me, I'd have been contented to be a bookkeeper." In keeping with that sentiment, to the perennial question "Which comes first, the music or the words?" Ira Gershwin always responded, "The contract."

By 1924, Gershwin had dropped the pseudonym Arthur Francis, and music by George and lyrics by Ira Gershwin would become a mainstay of popular music. From 1924 until George Gershwin's premature death in 1937, they wrote almost exclusively with each other, composing more than two dozen scores for Broadway and Hollywood, "elevating musical comedy to an American art form."

Lady Be Good (1924) was followed by successes including *Tip Toes, Oh, Kay!** *Funny Face, Rosalie, Show Girl* and *Girl Crazy*. Their show titles conformed to George's superstition that titles should have no more than two words and should, if possible, have something to do with a girl. This notion was abandoned with the success of the shows *Strike Up the Band* and *Of Thee I Sing*.†

In 1931, Ira Gershwin shared the Pulitzer Prize with George S. Kaufman and Morris Ryskind for *Of Thee I Sing*, the first musical to win the Pulitzer Prize for Drama. Although George had written the musical score, Ira was the only one recognized as the winner for his lyrics. After this award, all Pulitzers awarded to musicals would include the composers as well as the lyricists.

Of Thee I Sing was followed by *An American in Paris* (1928) and *Girl Crazy* (1930). In 1935, the Gershwin brothers, with DuBose Heyward, wrote the words and music for *Porgy and Bess*, the now classic folk opera. The Gershwin brothers insisted on hiring only Black singers to play the parts in the opera at a time when blackface entertainment was still common. Many consider *Porgy and Bess* the greatest American opera written.

Following the Broadway production of *Porgy and Bess*, Gershwin spent most of his time in Hollywood working on motion pictures, including the 1943 score for Samuel Goldwyn's *The North Star*. Although the film was nominated for six Academy Awards, the script would land the filmmaker before the House Un-American Activities Committee (HUAC) because of its alleged pro-Soviet theme.

Ira Gershwin's brother and collaborator George died in 1937 at the age of thirty-eight from a brain tumor while writing the music for *The Goldwyn Follies*. Ira completed the score for the movie, but once done, he shut himself off from the world for three years until the playwright Moss Hart convinced him to collaborate with Kurt Weill to write the lyrics for *Lady in the Dark*. This

---

* "Someone to Watch Over Me," written for the show *Oh, Kay!*, has been this author's favorite song since she was seven years old.
† Not to be overshadowed by George's idiosyncrasies, Ira avoided ending his lines with *d*, *t*, *b*, *k* or *f* sounds, which are harder to sing.

FESTIVAL '78 . . . Lyricist Ira and his brother, composer George Gershwin, caricatured here by Hirschfeld, are the subject of a television tribute during FESTIVAL '78 on PBS, 16 days of special programming designed to increase public awareness and support of public television. "Song by Song by Ira Gershwin" will air on ———————— at ———.
(Please check local listings for exact date and time in your area.)

Ira and George Gershwin depicted in a Hirshfeld cartoon.

was followed by *Cover Girl* (1944), which featured the song "Long Ago and Far Away," which was nominated for an Academy Award. The song sold more copies of sheet music in one year than any other song.

Ira Gershwin's final score for *A Star Is Born* was released in 1954, with music by Harold Arlen.* Gershwin was introduced to Judy Garland when she was cast as Dorothy in *The Wizard of Oz*. "The Man Who Got Away," written for Garland, brought Gershwin his third Academy Award nomination.

Ira Gershwin died in 1983 at eighty-six years of age. One month before he died, New York's largest theater, The Uris, was renamed to honor George and

---

* Harold Arlen was the composer of the score for *The Wizard of Oz*, with Gershwin's old friend and CCNY alumni Yip Harburg.

Ira and George Gershwin official postage stamp, 1999.

Ira Gershwin. Now known as The Gershwin, it has nearly 1,900 seats. *Wicked* opened at The Gershwin in 2003 and has been running there ever since.

In 1985, Congress recognized the legacy of George and Ira Gershwin by posthumously awarding them the Congressional Gold Medal. This was only the third time in U.S. history that a songwriter had been so honored.

In 1987, Ira's widow established the Ira Gershwin Literacy Center at University Settlement on the Lower East Side of New York. University Settlement is the oldest settlement house in the United States. The center is designed to give English-language programs to primarily Hispanic and Chinese Americans. Ira and George Gershwin spent many hours at University Settlement, located on Eldridge Street, where in 1896 Ira was born in a walk-up tenement.

In 1996, Ira Gershwin was the first lyricist to be honored by a special tribute performance on the centennial observance of his birth at New York's Carnegie Hall.

In 1999, six U.S. postage stamps, part of the Legends of American Music series, were issued, including a stamp with the faces of George and Ira Gershwin.

The Library of Congress Gershwin Prize for Popular Song, created in 2007, is awarded to a composer or performer for their lifetime contributions to popular music. The first prize was awarded to Paul Simon in 2007. Lionel Richie was the 2022 honoree. In the Gershwin Room of the Library of Congress, visitors can see George's piano and Ira's typewriter on display.

In 2022, the lyrics of Ira Gershwin can still be heard from Muncie, Indiana, to Paris, France, in productions of *An American in Paris* and *Porgy and Bess*.

Edgar Yipsel Harburg

CCNY
BS, 1921

"Brother, Can You Spare a Dime?," written by Yip Harburg, was the anthem of the Great Depression. While the song is credited with ensuring the passage of New Deal legislation for Franklin Roosevelt, it was not Harburg's most famous or lasting ballad.

Isadore Hochberg, the son of Russian immigrants, was born into poverty on Manhattan's Lower East Side in 1896, the youngest of four surviving children (out of ten). His parents, who never learned to speak English, and his elder sister worked in sweatshops, earning less than three cents an hour and working fourteen to sixteen hours a day. At twelve years old, Hochberg took a job lighting streetlamps at dusk and then getting up at 3:00 a.m. to turn them off. It was in this environment that the dream of Democratic Socialism took root in Isadore, who by this time was known as Edgar Hochberg and later Yip Harburg.*

Despite the circumstances of his youth, Harburg's parents ensured that he was exposed to art, culture and religion. His appreciation for art and culture would last his lifetime. After the loss of his elder brother to cancer and then his mother, Harburg became an agnostic. According to Harburg, "The House of G-d never had much appeal for me....Anyhow, I found a substitute temple—the theater."

As a child, Harburg saved up change earned from a series of menial jobs and watched the vaudeville acts of young entertainers like Al Jolson, Ed

---

* A dedicated socialist, Harburg's nickname "Yip" represents his politics. He became Yip not for his Yiddish name Yipsel but for YPSL, an acronym for Young People's Socialist League.

Wynn and Bert Lahr. Lahr would cross paths with Harburg years later when Lahr would make famous the role of the Cowardly Lion in *The Wizard of Oz*, written for him by Harburg.

Books were Harburg's escape from day-to-day poverty, and education was his way out of poverty. His introduction to the world outside of the tenements of the Lower East Side was driven by a very practical need to keep warm. Harburg's family lived in a cold-water flat heated by a small coal stove. To keep warm, Harburg would go to the library on Thompkins Square and 10th Street, where the librarians introduced him to a world of words and books that would last a lifetime.

After elementary school, Harburg attended Townsend Harris High School, where a three-year education led directly to a four-year program at CCNY. At Townsend Harris, Harburg was an editor of the school's newspaper, co-editing a column called "Much Ado" with a classmate named Isidore Gershvin, later to be known to the world as Ira Gershwin. They bonded after sitting next to each other in homeroom thanks to alphabetical seating and discovered a shared appreciation for Gilbert and Sullivan and a hatred of algebra. Both Harburg and Gershwin attended CCNY, where according to Harburg, "You didn't have to pay any fee, you didn't have to pay for textbooks. It was a wonderful place." Many years later, Harburg and Gershwin would collaborate on the Broadway show *Life Begins at 8:40*.

While CCNY was free, Harburg had to work selling newspapers and groceries and any job he could find to help support his parents. His grades, especially in math and science, reflected this. According to Harburg, "There was no such thing as a vacation, and no such thing as seeing a tree or anything like that or taking a swim." Harburg's goal, like most students' at CCNY, was to graduate as soon as possible and get a job. According to Harburg, "When you got the diploma, it didn't mean a damn thing either. Now, what do you do with that?"

In 1918, before graduating from CCNY, Harburg was sidetracked by a job he could not turn down and a war he wanted to avoid. With only twenty-one credits left to graduate, Harburg accepted a job in Swift and Company's Uruguay office. This allowed him to avoid fighting in World War I, and according to Harburg, "It was the first time I was able to support my mother and father which was what I wanted." Three years later, he returned to New York and got a job with Consolidated Gas and Electric Company, where he had worked as a child turning streetlights on and off. He attended evening classes at CCNY, and unlike his friend Ira Gershwin, who dropped out, Harburg graduated from CCNY in 1921 with a Bachelor of Science degree.

A songbook featuring Yip Harburg's greatest hits.

After leaving his job at Consolidated Gas and Electric Company, Harburg founded an electrical appliance company and quickly achieved success and wealth. But neither was a substitute for the happiness he found in writing verse. According to Harburg, "For the next few years, we made a lot of money, and I hated it. But the economy saved me. The capitalists saved me in 1929, just as we were worth, oh, about a quarter of a million dollars. Bang! The whole thing blew up. I was left with a pencil and finally had to write for a living." As he told Studs Terkel, "What the Depression was for most people was for me a lifesaver." Harburg's company went bankrupt following the 1929 crash, leaving him anywhere from $50,000 to $70,000 in debt, which he paid back over the course of the next several decades.

To quote Harburg, "I left the fantasy of business for the harsh reality of musical theatre." His friend Ira Gershwin would be there with an introduction to a songwriting career and a loan. In 1932, Harburg's break would come when he collaborated with Jay Gourney on *Americana*. Unlike the movies and Broadway shows of the time, which reflected a distraction from the Depression, Harburg's songs were about the common man and the America of unemployment, breadlines and poverty. The most well known of the songs Harburg wrote during this time was "Brother, Can You Spare a Dime?" The song's lament would resonate throughout the entire body of his work. The song was a hit with both audiences and critics, though not without pushback. While it became the informal anthem of Roosevelt's New Deal, Republican opposition thought that the song was anti-capitalist propaganda. This political refrain would come to haunt Harburg in the decades to follow.

Between 1929 and 1934, Harburg worked with thirty-one composers, including Arthur Schwartz, Dana Suesse, Burton Lane and Harold Arlen. His collaboration with Arlen led to the popular song "It's Only a Paper Moon." In 1939, the collaboration led to their most well-known project, a movie musical based on L. Frank Baum's *The Wonderful Wizard of Oz*, reuniting Harburg with Ed Wynn, the actor Harburg had watched on the vaudeville stage when he was a child.

The title song from *The Wizard of Oz*, "Somewhere Over the Rainbow," would become one of the most famous songs of all time. Yet it was not a part of the original movie screenplay, nor was it part of Baum's book. It was a device invented by Harburg as a symbol for the colors unseen by Dorothy in her black-and-white world. In addition to writing the lyrics to all the songs in *The Wizard of Oz*, Harburg was the final script editor for the movie. This was the first time that music would be integrated into a story and the story would not stop for a song to be sung. In 1940, "Somewhere Over the Rainbow" won the Academy Award for Best Song.

The Wizard of Oz was followed in 1943 by *Cabin in the Sky*, the first all-Black musical to be adapted to film. *Cabin in the Sky* was nominated for the Academy Award for Best Music, Original Song. In 1944, Harburg and Arlen again collaborated, this time on *Bloomer Girl*, which addressed the horrors of the Civil War, slavery and women's suffrage.

Harburg's best-known Broadway show, *Finian's Rainbow*,* a collaboration with Burton Lane in 1947, would again make a statement about racism and injustice in America. It would break precedent with a racially integrated cast and chorus. Its plot satirized American financial practices and criticized the mistreatment of the working classes, as well as racism and Jim Crow laws in America.

In 1950, Harburg was summoned to appear before the House Un-American Activities Committee (HUAC). Harburg had been named in *Red Channels*, a pamphlet distributed to organizations involved in employing people in the entertainment industry. The pamphlet listed 150 people who had been involved in promoting left-wing causes.

The actor Robert Taylor, who was a friendly witness at the HUAC hearings, complained that the lyrics of Harburg's songs were radical, to which Harburg responded, "As a firm, almost fanatical believer in democracy, as a proud American, and as the writer of the lyric of the song 'God's Country,' I am outraged by the suggestion that somehow I am connected with, believe in, or am sympathetic with Communist or totalitarian philosophy. Guilt by association is a European doctrine which has always been repudiated in this country, and it is about time that decent liberals and good Americans fought back against this European theory."

As a result of the blacklist, the movie *Finian's Rainbow*, starring Fred Astaire and Petula Clark and directed by Francis Ford Coppola, was not filmed until 1968.

---

* The song "How Are Things in Glocca Morra" was playing in 1948 when a young congressman, John F. Kennedy, learned that his sister Kathleen had been killed in a plane crash in France.

The cast of *The Wizard of Oz*, which featured the classic Yip Harburg song "Over the Rainbow."

Although not a communist, Harburg was blacklisted from motion pictures, television and radio from 1951 to 1962. After two years without work in Hollywood, Harburg returned to New York, where he testified before the International Alliance for Theatrical Stage Employees to discuss

Yip Harburg official postage stamp, 2005.

removing his name from the blacklist. The organization apparently had a file on him and wanted to know if the "Joe" in his hit song "Happiness Is a Thing Called Joe" referred to Joe Stalin.

Throughout the 1960s and '70s, Harburg wrote books of light satirical verses and performed narrated concerts. In 1966, he collaborated with Earl Robinson for the song "Hurray Sundown," recorded by Peter, Paul and Mary. The song was nominated for the Grammy Award for Best Folk Recording.

Over his career, Harburg wrote the lyrics to more than six hundred songs. A poll conducted by the Recording Industry Association of America and the National Endowment for the Humanities ranked Judy Garland's rendition of "Over the Rainbow" as the no. 1 recording in the twentieth century. In 2004, the American Film Institute listed the one hundred greatest film songs, and "Over the Rainbow" was ranked no. 1.

Yip Harburg died in 1981 at eighty-four years of age. Like his famous song, through his music, Harburg never stopped looking for that place somewhere over the rainbow where people dared to dream.

In 2005, the U.S. Postal Service issued the Yip Harburg commemorative stamp. The original image was that of Harburg's portrait. After the fact, the artist who designed the stamp added a rainbow and a lyric fragment from Harburg's Oscar-winning song.

FRANK LOESSER

CCNY
ATTENDED 1925

Frank Loesser would win accolades from his peers and the public but never from his parents or his family. Although he won four Tony Awards and the Pulitzer Prize, he was always considered the black sheep in the family.

Frank Loesser was born in 1910 in New York City. His father was a distinguished teacher of classical piano, and his elder brother was a renowned concert pianist. Recognizing his innate talent, Loesser's father noted that at only four years old, his son could play "any tune he heard by ear." Despite his father's insistence and much to his father's dismay, Frank refused to study classical music.

Loesser's interest was in popular music, writing his first song at the age of six ("The May Party"). Forgoing the opportunities his upbringing offered him, Loesser taught himself how to play the piano and the harmonica, winning third place in a citywide harmonica contest, much to the disdain of his family. According to his daughter, Susan Loesser, his family "considered his ability very nice but not music." Loesser would make it his life's mission to prove his family wrong.

Loesser attended Townsend Harris High School. In 1925, he was expelled from CCNY after his father died, forcing him to seek work to support his family. Loesser worked as an ad salesman for the *New York Herald Tribune*, a political cartoonist, a process server and, his favorite job, city editor of a short-lived newspaper in New Rochelle until he found his niche writing jingles. During the day, he wrote jingles for $100 per week. None was published. As Loesser called it, "These early years were a rendezvous with failure."

In 1931, Loesser teamed with William Schuman, who later became president of Juilliard. They wrote "In Love with a Memory of You," Loesser's first published lyric. Schuman later said, "Frank Loesser has written hits with

Hoagy Carmichael, Burton Lane, Jule Styne and other Hollywood grand dukes, but I have the distinction of having written a flop with him."

During this time, Loesser earned a living by singing and playing piano in nightclubs, while he wrote lyrics to music written by Irving Actman. The duo contributed five songs to *The Illustrator's Show*, which opened in 1936 and closed after five performances. Although a failure, the collaboration resulted in a Hollywood contract for Loesser, first at Universal Studios and then Paramount, despite the concern of the studio heads that Loesser's lyrics had an edge that might have to be censored.

At Paramount, Loesser wrote his first hit song for a Dorothy Lamour movie, *Hurricane*. Among the well-known songs for which Loesser provided the words during these years were "Two Sleepy People" and "Heart and Soul," with Hoagy Carmichael.

Loesser remained in Hollywood until World War II intervened, and he enlisted in the U.S. Army Air Force. While he was in the armed services, the

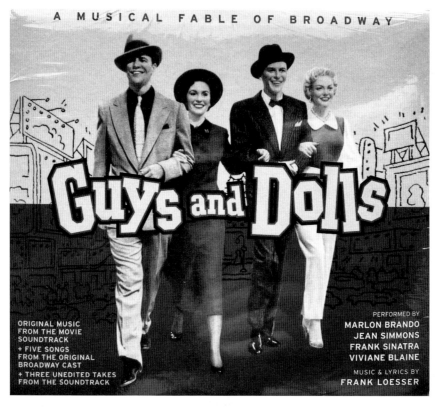

Guys and Dolls, with music and lyrics by Frank Loesser. This iconic version starred Frank Sinatra and Marlon Brando.

army began producing musicals designed for soldiers to perform in the field. The musicals were known as "Blueprint Specials." Between 1944 and 1945, most of the songs for these shows were written by Loesser, including the popular "Praise the Lord and Pass the Ammunition," which was for World War II what "Over There" had been for World War I.

At the end of World War II, Loesser returned to Hollywood for a short time, writing the words and music to songs such as "What Are You Doing New Year's Eve?" and "On a Slow Boat to China." He would eventually write lyrics to songs for more than sixty films, including *Destry Rides Again* and *Let's Dance*, starring Fred Astaire. But his first love was the stage.

Despite his success writing songs for movies, Loesser wanted to "create situations" rather than songs. "Songwriting is a little thing and I settled for a big thing, the Broadway musical." In the words of Oscar Levant, "In Hollywood, he was a cog in the wheel. He didn't have control over what was done with his songs. He turned them in and then the producers took them and did as they pleased. On Broadway, the composer had control."

At the encouragement of producers Cy Feuer and Ernest Martin, Loesser returned to Broadway to write the lyrics and music for *Where's Charley*. The show opened on October 11, 1948, and became Loesser's first major hit. *Where's Charley* won the 1949 Tony Award for Best Actor and ran for 792 performances. Loesser would no longer be seen by his critics as merely a writer of popular songs for movies. With *Where's Charley*, Loesser created a musical score integrated into a story as part of a Broadway show. Loesser would never write a standalone song again.

In 1948, Loesser sold a song to MGM he wrote in 1944 for the movie *Neptune's Daughter*. The song was "Baby, It's Cold Outside." The backstory and the end story of this song could have been the setting for a Broadway play with music and lyrics by Loesser. "Baby, It's Cold Outside" was originally written by Loesser to sing with his wife to indicate to guests that it was time to leave a housewarming party. According to Loesser, "We became instant parlor room stars. We got invited to all the best parties for years on the basis of 'Baby.'" The song won the 1950 Academy Award for Best Original Song. In the movie *Neptune's Daughter*, there were two versions of the song. In the first version, the woman wants to leave, and the man, who is the host, tries to stop her. In the second version, a parody of the first, the man wants to leave, and the woman, who is the hostess, wants him to stay. The humor of the two versions of the song was lost in the early 2000s when a new generation attempted to "cancel" the holiday standard by sounding the alarm of the Me Too movement. As of 2020, there were more than four hundred recordings of "Baby, It's Cold Outside."

In the late 1940s, Loesser formed his own music publishing company, Frank Music Corporation. The primary purpose was to develop new composers and lyricists. In 1976, Frank Music was acquired by CBS, and today it is a part of Paul McCartney's music publishing company, MPL Communications.

Loesser's biggest hit was yet to come when, in 1950, Cy Feuer and Ernest Martin, the producers of *Where's Charley*, approached Loesser to write the music and lyrics to the Damon Runyon story

How to Succeed in Business without Really Trying,
with music and lyrics by Frank Loesser.

about a group of Hell's Kitchen gamblers. The story would become *Guys and Dolls*. Loesser suited each song to the character who performed it. After 1,200 performances, *Guys and Dolls* swept the 1951 Tony Awards with Best Musical (Frank Loesser), Best Actor, Best Actress, Best Choreography and Best Director. Loesser's songs for *Guys and Dolls* include "I'll Know When My Love Comes Along," "Sit Down, You're Rocking the Boat," "A Bushel and a Peck," "I've Never Been in Love Before," "Luck Be a Lady," "Take Back Your Mink" and "If I Were a Bell."

In the following decade, Loesser wrote the book, music and lyrics for *The Most Happy Fella* and the music and lyrics for *Hans Christian Andersen* and *Greenwillow*, earning him two more Tony nominations and a Drama Critics Award.

In 1961, Loesser again collaborated with producers Cy Feuer and Ernest Martin, writing the music and lyrics for *How to Succeed in Business without Really Trying*. The show won the 1962 Pulitzer Prize for Drama, seven Tony Awards and the Grammy for Best Musical Theater Album. It ran for 1,417 shows and was revived twice on Broadway, in 1995 and in 2011. President Kennedy had the album in his White House record collection. According to Mimi Alford in her 2012 memoir, "The President was especially fond of the way Robert Morse sang the lines 'being a seeker of wisdom and truth' from the song 'I Believe in You.'" *How to Succeed in Business without Really Trying* became the longest running of any of Loesser's shows and at that time only the fourth musical to win a Pulitzer Prize. (Currently, ten musicals have won a Pulitzer Prize, including, most recently, *Hamilton*.)

Frank Loesser official postage stamp, 1999.

According to reviewer John D. Shout, "Frank Loesser achieved what every artist most covets: the esteem of his colleagues." Richard Rodgers called Loesser "a man for all theater seasons," while Bob Fosse regarded *Guys and Dolls* as simply "the greatest American musical of all time." Paddy Chayefsky remarked that "he [Loesser] introduced reality and sanity into the musical comedy."

Frank Loesser died of lung cancer in 1968. He was fifty-nine years old. "The evil of two Loessers," as his brother called him, achieved greatness that far surpassed his accomplished family members. That greatness was memorialized when in 1999 Frank Loesser, along with other songwriters like George and Ira Gershwin, was honored by the U.S. Postal Service with a postage stamp bearing his likeness.

Chapter 6
PERFORMING ARTS

Edward G. Robinson

CCNY
Attended 1914

Edward G. Robinson was born in 1893, but he liked to say, "Life for me began when I was 10 years old." It was on that date that he and his family landed on Ellis Island.

Born Emanuel Goldenberg in Bucharest, Romania, Robinson, his parents and his four brothers came to America after a brother became a victim of an anti-Semitic attack and was left permanently brain damaged.

Robinson and his family settled on the Lower East Side of New York City. Hebrew, Romanian and German were spoken at home. This facility in foreign languages would benefit Robinson many times, the first time being when he mastered the English language before entering public school.

As an adolescent, Robinson spent hours at the Astor Place Library, reciting speeches to anyone who would listen. His favorite was Theodore Roosevelt's second inaugural speech, which included the line, "Much has been given us, and much will rightfully be expected from us."

Robinson attended Townsend Harris High School, hoping to pursue a career as a criminal lawyer "to defend the human beings who were abused and exploited." Little did Robinson know that in his case art would not imitate life, and he would make a career playing criminals on screen.

Edward G. Robinson.

While Robinson entered CCNY intending to study law, he found his passion as an actor. After earning a scholarship to the American Academy of Dramatic Arts, he was advised to change his name. Emanuel Goldenberg became Edward G. Robinson, the "G" standing for the last name of his birth. When his unconventional looks were seen as a liability, Robinson replied, "Some people have youth, others beauty, I have menace."

Like many Jewish actors of the time, Robinson's acting career began in the Yiddish Theater District. Unlike many, it was not long before he would make his Broadway debut. In 1915, Robinson debuted in the show *Under Fire*, a role that called for someone who was multilingual. His film debut in *Arms and the Women* soon followed.

Robinson was a major stage actor, having twenty-nine Broadway plays to his credit before he arrived in Hollywood. In 1923, after serving in the army during World War I, Robinson appeared in the silent film *The Bright Shawl* under the name E.G. Robinson. This would be his first credited role, although not under the name he would soon make famous.

Unlike many actors of the time, Robinson made a seamless transition to talking films, making fourteen talking films between 1930 and 1932. His breakthrough role was in 1931 as the gangster Caesar Enrico Bandello in *Little Caesar*, a role that would define Edward G. Robinson.

Robinson's next breakthrough role was in 1939 in *Confessions of a Nazi Spy*, the first movie that portrayed Nazis as a threat to America.

In 1942, at the outset of World War II, Robinson volunteered to serve in the U.S. military but was denied active service due to his age. He was forty-eight years old. This rejection didn't stop him from participating in the war effort as an outspoken critic of fascism and Nazism. In July 1944, Robinson was the first movie star to travel to Normandy to entertain troops for the USO. He donated an entire year's earnings to the USO and subsequently donated another $100,000 (equivalent to $1.8 million today), his entire earnings from his role in the 1948 film *Larceny*. Because of his fluency in several languages, the Office of War Information recruited Robinson to read encouraging messages to U.S. troops in occupied Europe.

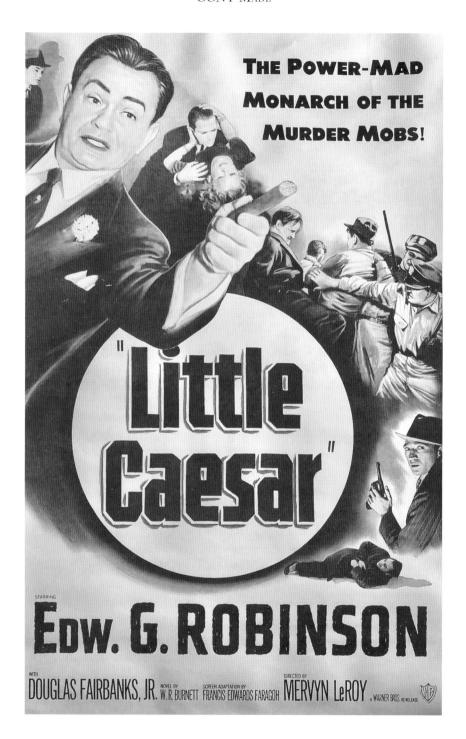

Opposite: *Little Caesar*, starring Edward G. Robinson and Douglas Fairbanks Jr.

Above: Edward G. Robinson official postage stamp, 2000.

Robinson's generosity to more than 850 organizations (he donated more than $250,000 or more than $3 million in today's dollars) in support of the war effort had unintended consequences when he was called to testify before the House Un-American Activities Committee (HUAC) in 1950 and 1952. Robinson named names the committee already had, including Dalton Trumbo. Robinson would go on to lend Trumbo and his family money when Trumbo was blacklisted and imprisoned. The committee concluded that it never had any evidence to indicate that Robinson was "anything more than a sucker."

Although exonerated by HUAC, Robinson was "gray-listed." Roles in Hollywood were not forthcoming. An ugly divorce resulted in Robinson having to sell his collection of art, including works by Pissarro, Monet, Cézanne, Renoir and Van Gogh for $3.25 million in 1956 ($10.9 million in today's dollars).

Robinson found himself relegated to supporting parts, reminiscent of when in his youth he would tell casting agents, "I'm not so much on face value, but when it comes to stage value, I'll deliver for you." In 1956, he did just that, returning to Broadway and earning a 1956 Tony Award nomination for Best Actor in *Middle of the Night*, written by Paddy Chayefsky, another CCNY alumni.

Robinson appeared in thirty Broadway plays and more than one hundred films during his fifty-year career. He is ranked number twenty-four in the American Film Institute's list of twenty-five greatest male stars of classic American cinema.

Edward G. Robinson died in 1973 at eighty years of age. He was awarded an Honorary Academy Award for his work in the film industry two months after he died. In October 2000, Robinson's image was imprinted on a U.S. postage stamp.

In 2009, the *Guardian* named him one of the best actors never to have received an Academy Award nomination, notwithstanding his Honorary Award.

Edward G. Robinson was educated, cultured, multilingual, a major collector of fine art and well known for his generosity. The man, like his name, was so very different from the parts he played that made him famous.

Zero Mostel

CCNY
BA, 1935

The world remembers him as "Zero," a man who began with nothing, like Tevye, the character he made famous in *Fiddler on the Roof*.

Samuel Joel Mostel was born in 1915. His parents, who emigrated from Europe, settled on the Lower East Side of Manhattan and raised eight children. Samuel's father, Israel, helped the Jewish community with religious matters, while his mother, Celia, wrote and translated letters for neighbors who struggled with English. The family had enough money for only basic things. But they had dreams for their children.

Israel Mostel wanted his son Samuel to become a rabbi. But Samuel wanted to be an artist, an ambition that his mother supported. Celia sent her son to the Metropolitan Museum of Art dressed in a velvet suit, armed with paper and pencils, so he could copy the great masterpieces housed at

Zero Mostel's promo portrait for Mel Brooks's *The Producers*.

the museum. "Look at Sam," she would say, "a child and he draws like a man."

While Mostel attended PS 188, his mother made sure his public education was supplemented with classes at the Educational Alliance, an institution founded to provide Jewish immigrants in New York with cultural enrichment.

In 1928, Mostel enrolled in Seward Park High School. His grades ranged from a low of 55 to a high of 95. He graduated in 1931. Below his senior yearbook photo reads the inscription, "A future Rembrandt…or perhaps a comedian?"

Mostel enrolled at CCNY, where he majored in fine arts and English. There were a limited number of art classes offered, so Mostel took the same classes twice to learn as much as he could from each professor.

While at CCNY, Mostel developed two personalities: the private, stoic artist who learned everything he could in class and the zany comic. When his friend Sam Levene learned that Mostel was playing the lead role in CCNY's production of *Hamlet*, Levene told Mostel, "A big, fat, horrible-looking slob like you as the Melancholy Dane? What kind of typecasting is that?" Mostel replied, "I am the *ideal* Hamlet! Shakespeare describes Hamlet as 'fat and scant of breath' and gahdamit, there's nobody fatter or scanter of breath than me." This was Zero's first time onstage but not his last.

In 1935, Mostel graduated from CCNY with a bachelor's degree. He named this year "the year of the miracles." In pursuit of an artistic career, he took night classes at New York University while working odd jobs during the day. After a year, he dropped out of NYU. "The artist must *do* things," he said. In truth, Mostel had no idea what to do.

During the Depression, with jobs scarce, life was bleak for Mostel until Congress approved the Works Progress Administration (WPA) and the Federal Art Project (FAP). These programs paid artists to paint murals, teach and give free tours of galleries and museums around New York City. In 1937, Mostel became the youngest artist hired by FAP.

From 1937 to 1939, Mostel earned $23.86 each week teaching classes in beginner and intermediate painting at the 92nd Street Young Men's and Young Women's Hebrew Association. At the same time, he gave talks at the Frick, the Museum of Modern Art and the Museum of Science and Industry. During these talks, Mostel honed his skills as a comedian.

In 1941, after listening to one of Mostel's museum talks, Ivan Black, a press agent, approached Mostel and asked him where he worked. Mostel replied, "In the studio." Black asked which one, Paramount or Twentieth Century. "Are you kidding?" said Mostel. "In my own studio. I paint pictures." This would become Mostel's opening line as a stand-up comic.

Black invited Mostel to audition with the owner of Café Society Downtown. He was a flop. After several months, Mostel was brought back to reaudition, and this time he was hired. At the suggestion of Black, Samuel Mostel adopted the stage name "Zero." "After all," said Black, "here's a guy who's starting from zero." On February 16, 1942, Samuel Mostel left his job with FAP and made his professional debut as Zero Mostel, comedian, at Café Society Downtown.

Mostel may have started from zero, but he didn't stay there long. With his growing popularity, his weekly salary increased from $40 to $100 to $450. Mostel began appearing on radio programs like *The Chamber Music Society of Lower Basin Street* and Broadway shows including *Keep 'Em Laughing* and *Top Notchers*. Zero Mostel quickly became a household name.

Mostel was drafted in 1943 to serve in the U.S. Army. After being discharged, he entertained servicemen through the USO. In 1945, Mostel returned to stand-up comedy in New York and eventually the movies. His cinematic works include *Panic in the Streets* (1950), *The Guy Who Came Back* (1951), *The Enforcer* (1951) and *The Model and the Marriage Broker* (1951). But success would not last long.

In 1955, Mostel was subpoenaed by the House Un-American Activities Committee (HUAC) after he was accused of being a communist. To avoid self-incrimination and "naming names," Mostel invoked the Fifth Amendment. As a result, his name was added to the government blacklist of alleged communists, and he was denied work in the United States. Mostel later quipped, "What did they think I was going to do—sell acting secrets to the Russians?"

While he was applauded by fellow actors for not naming names, for several years Mostel could not find work in the theater or in movies. To survive, Mostel performed at small venues for little pay. In 1958, work resurfaced when he was offered the leading role in Burgess Meredith's off-Broadway production of *Ulysses in Nighttown*. The production earned Mostel an Obie Award. One year later, Mostel made his television debut in *The World of Sholem Aleichem*.

In 1959, Mostel again faced what would have been a catastrophic setback for a less determined person. He was about to star in the Broadway production of *The Good Soup* when he was hit by a bus, and his left leg was

Newsweek

OCTOBER 19, 1964   35c

Zero Mostel

Broadway's Brightest Star

Zero Mostel as Tevye in the original Broadway production of *Fiddler on the Roof*, depicted on the cover of *Newsweek*, 1964.

crushed. Initially, he was told that his leg had to be amputated. Fortunately, before the operation he was transferred to the Hospital for Joint Diseases, where the director of surgery was able to save his leg. During a five-month recovery, Mostel entertained the staff. According to the man who saved

Mostel's leg, "Everybody at the hospital loved Zero, not only because he was so funny and charming, but because the man was fantastically brave....The man is truly astonishing."

After his recovery, Mostel returned to the Broadway stage and won his first Tony Award for his performance in Eugène Ionesco's *Rhinoceros*. Mostel earned a second Tony Award for his role in *A Funny Thing Happened on the Way to the Forum* and a third Tony Award for originating the iconic role of Tevye the dairyman in the Broadway success *Fiddler on the Roof*. With three Tony Awards in five years, when audiences saw his name on a theater marquee, they knew that the show would be a success.

In his later years, Mostel returned to film, reprising some of his most famous Broadway roles on screen. He also added new characters to his repertoire such as Max Bialystock in Mel Brooks's (another CCNY alumni) *The Producers* (1968). In 1976, Mostel appeared in his last film, *The Front*, in which he played the role of a blacklisted comedian, a role he knew well.

In 1977, Zero was cast as one of the leading roles in a new Shakespeare reimagining called *The Merchant*. The tryout performance was halted when Mostel fell ill. Mostel would never grace the stage again. On September 8, 1977, Zero Mostel died of a heart attack. He was sixty-two.

Max Bialystock in *The Producers* lamented, "Where did we go right?" Samuel Joel "Zero" Mostel went very right. He became a legend in his own time despite rejection, blacklisting and injury. He laughed at himself, and his audience laughed with him.

Tony Curtis

CCNY
Attended 1945–1946

"I was a million-to-one shot, the least likely to succeed. I wasn't low man on the totem pole, I was under the totem pole, in a sewer, tied to a sack." This is how Tony Curtis saw his life. The Oscar nominee best known for his good looks and Bronx accent could not have been more wrong.

Tony Curtis was born Bernard Schwartz in 1925 to Hungarian immigrants. His family lived in the Bronx in a two-room apartment in the back of his father's tailor shop, his parents living in one room and Curtis and his two brothers in the other room.

Curtis described his childhood as "the school of hard knocks." His mother beat her three sons during episodes of schizophrenia. His youngest brother, who also suffered from schizophrenia, was institutionalized. When Curtis was seven years old, his parents let him know that he was responsible for his three-year-old brother, Julius, a role Curtis embraced. When Curtis was thirteen years old, Julius was hit and killed by a truck, and Curtis was called on as next of kin to identify his younger brother's body. When his parents could not provide for Curtis and his brothers, the brothers were placed in a state-run orphanage for a month.

Because only Hungarian was spoken in the Schwartz household, starting school was delayed for Curtis until he was six. While school was a haven for many first-generation American children, Curtis was constantly bullied by his peers with anti-Semitic taunts. At eleven, he joined a neighborhood gang and began skipping school and committing petty crimes. As Curtis recalled, he learned to dodge the stones and fists to protect his face, which he realized even then would be his ticket out of the Bronx.

The first light in his otherwise bleak childhood came when a neighbor sent Curtis to Boy Scout camp. By this time, Curtis realized that he could only depend on himself: "Over time I learned to cope, mostly by realizing that I couldn't count on anyone else, which later on would have the unexpected benefit of making me resourceful and independent."

To get away from the horror of his home life and torments by his peers, Curtis escaped to the movies. "My whole culture as a boy was movies," Curtis said. "For 11 cents you could sit in the front row of a theater for 10 hours, which I did constantly. As a kid I longed to see myself ten feet tall on the big screen."

Curtis began taking his future seriously when he attended Seward Park High School. This was short-lived, as at sixteen Curtis enlisted in the U.S. Navy after the attack on Pearl Harbor. Because he was under eighteen, he forged his mother's signature on the permission form. The navy became his surrogate family. He learned Morse code and was promoted to signalman third class. Curtis was honorably discharged in 1945, after the surrender of Japan.

Following his discharge from the navy, Curtis got a job as a truck driver and attended CCNY on the G.I. Bill, allowing him to go to acting school without paying for it. He also took acting classes at the New School for Social Research. Curtis auditioned for the New York Dramatic Workshop and was accepted on the strength of his audition, a scene from *Dr. Jekyll and Mr. Hyde* in pantomime. In 1948, while performing in the Catskills, he drew the attention of talent agent Joyce Selznick, the niece of film producer David O Selznick. This led to a seven-year contract with Universal Pictures. Bernard Schwartz became Tony Curtis, a name that Bernie Schwartz saw as "elegant and mysterious."

Curtis's first film was an uncredited two-minute role in *Criss Cross*. In 1950, he had roles in three westerns, was billed under his newly adopted name and received so many fan letters that in 1951 Curtis was given the starring role in *The Prince Who Was a Thief*. His next hit was in 1953 playing opposite his wife, Janet Leigh, in *Houdini*, a movie about another Hungarian Jewish entertainer, albeit a world-famous magician.

In 1955, Curtis and Janet Leigh formed their own independent production company and produced movies starring Curtis such as *The Vikings*, where Curtis made it seem natural for a Norseman to have a Bronx accent. Curtis's acting career began to flourish after he starred with Burt Lancaster in *Trapeze* and the following year in *Sweet Smell of Success*. The films received lackluster reviews, but Curtis enjoyed critical praise.

By 1956, Curtis wanted to act in movies that had social relevance. His chance came in 1958 when he starred in *The Defiant Ones*. Curtis broke a Hollywood taboo by insisting that an African American actor, Sidney Poitier, have co-star billing. Curtis played a white southern bigot chained to a Black man played by Poitier. *The Defiant Ones* won nine Oscar nominations, and for his role as an escaped convict, Curtis earned his only Oscar nomination for Best Actor.

In 1959, Curtis took a detour from dramatic roles and starred in the comedy *Some Like It Hot* alongside Jack Lemmon and Marilyn Monroe. This would be one of his most memorable performances. About working with Marilyn Monroe, Curtis said, "You could tell she'd already been battered by life, and I found that she'd been in an orphanage, as I had, and that her mother was also schizophrenic....We both wanted to be in the movies, and that meant everything." In 2002, Curtis toured in the musical adaptation of *Some Like It Hot*, in which he played the role of the elder millionaire originated by Joe E. Brown in the film. This time, Curtis had the curtain line, "Nobody's perfect." In 2000, an American Film Institute survey of funniest films in history ranked *Some Like It Hot* at no. 1.

In 1960, Curtis co-starred in *Spartacus*, a movie that marked the end of the blacklist but the perpetuation of the stigma of homosexuality in Hollywood. It would be the climax of Curtis's movie career. Kirk Douglas, the lead actor in the movie, insisted that Dalton Trumbo be given credit as the movie's screenwriter, effectively ending the blacklist in Hollywood. Trumbo had been banned from the movie industry for ten years, during which he

Poster for the classic film *Some Like It Hot*, starring Marilyn Monroe, Jack Lemmon and Tony Curtis.

won two Academy Awards for Best Story under assumed names. But the Hollywood liberal mystique stopped at the credits, as according to Curtis one of the most important scenes, the bath scene between Curtis's character, Antoninus, and Laurence Olivier's character, Marcus, was cut before the movie's release.

Following the success of *Spartacus*, Curtis's popularity waned. According to Curtis, he and his wife, Janet Leigh, were considered "the darlings of the Hollywood media." With their divorce and his subsequent marriage to his seventeen-year-old co-star, Curtis's Hollywood star quickly faded. "When I first hit Hollywood, I had really made a splash. Now the phone was silent. It was as if I had died, only someone forgot to tell me about it."

Curtis made a final attempt as a dramatic actor with his role in *The Boston Strangler*. While he received a Golden Globe nomination, the role failed to reignite his career. His decline in movie roles corresponded with his addiction to cocaine and time spent at the Betty Ford Clinic.

After starring in more than 150 pictures, Curtis's final screen appearance came in 2008, when he played a small role in *David & Fatima*. His character's

Laurence Olivier and Tony Curtis in *Spartacus*.

name was Mr. Schwartz, apropos for a man who spent his life becoming Tony Curtis.

The end of Curtis's movie career marked the beginning of his career as a philanthropist and artist. Curtis and his daughter, actress Jamie Lee Curtis, helped fund the rebuilding of Budapest's Great Synagogue. Curtis also founded the Emanuel Foundation for Hungarian Culture. In thanks, the Hungarian government dubbed Curtis a Hungarian Knight. And capitalizing on his aptitude as an artist that he showed as a young boy, in the early 2000s Curtis established himself as a legitimate artist, his work being included in the permanent collection of the New York Museum of Modern Art.

Curtis, one of the last survivors of the Hollywood studio system, died in 2010 at the age of eighty-five. While his biggest regret was not winning an Oscar, five films he appeared in have been selected for the National Film Registry by the Library of Congress as being "culturally, historically or aesthetically" significant: *Winchester '73* (1950), *Sweet Smell of Success* (1957), *Some Like It Hot* (1959), *Spartacus* (1960) and *Rosemary's Baby* (1968).

In 2001, Tony Curtis was the subject of a two-month, twelve-film retrospective at the New York Museum of Modern Art. According to Jackson Arn of *The Forward*, "These films are a monument to a one-of-a-kind performer: a street kid disguised as a pretty-boy, a supporting actor trapped in a star's body, a handsome mutant who stood the test of time because he never really fit in."

At the writing of this book, upon receiving an Academy Award, Curtis's daughter, Jamie Lee Curtis, thanked her parents for making it possible for her to receive that honor. She also recognized that few in the audience remembered them.

BUTTERFLY McQUEEN

CCNY
BA, 1975

"Oh, Miss Scarlett! I don't know nothin 'bout birthin' babies!" These words, among the most memorable in movie history, were uttered by Butterfly McQueen as Prissy, the house maid, in *Gone with the Wind*. The words and the movie role would define McQueen's career but not her life or her legacy.

Butterfly McQueen was born Thelma McQueen in 1911, the daughter of a dockworker and a maid. The family lived in Tampa, Florida, until McQueen was five years old and her father deserted the family. To support herself and her daughter, McQueen's mother sent McQueen to live with an aunt in Augusta, Georgia, while she looked for full-time employment in cities up and down the East Coast. After her mother settled on a job as a cook in the Harlem section of New York City, McQueen joined her.

McQueen attended convent school, where her first acting experience was reciting books from the Bible. According to McQueen, "All I knew as a child was church, church, church." After high school, she studied nursing at the Lincoln Training Center in the Bronx until a teacher suggested that she think about acting as a profession, and she began studying dance, music and drama. In 1934, McQueen joined Venezuela Jones's Harlem-based Youth Theatre Group, where she made her stage debut as part of the Butterfly Ballet in *A Midsummer Night's Dream*. Thus Thelma became Butterfly.

By 1936, McQueen was on Broadway playing the maid in George Abbott's all-Black production of *Brown Sugar*. The play closed after four shows, but Butterfly was a success. She became a permanent member of

'GONE WITH THE WIND.' a David O. Selznick Technicolor Production released by Metro-Goldwyn-Mayer

Butterfly McQueen in a scene with Vivien Leigh in *Gone with the Wind*.

the Abbott Acting Company and was subsequently cast in two other Abbott productions: *Brother Rat* (1937) and *What a Life* (1938).

During *What a Life*'s run, a scout for film producer David O. Selznick recognized McQueen's talent and suggested she audition for *Gone with the Wind*, the most talked-about movie of the year. She took the screen test but

Left: Poster for of the award-winning *Gone with the Wind*.

Right: Butterfly McQueen (*left*) on the set of *Gone with the Wind*.

was initially rejected, being called too chubby. Selznick overrode the criticism and gave McQueen the part of Prissy, Scarlett O'Hara's slow-witted maid. As Prissy, Butterfly McQueen would utter one of the most memorable lines in cinema history.

According to film historian Donald Bogle, *Gone with the Wind* was "the first of the Civil War spectacles to provide a realistic picture of black-white relationships in antebellum America. It was also the first in which black actors were given the freedom to transform pasteboard slave characters into complex, three-dimensional human beings." Not all the Black actors agreed.

McQueen accepted the role of Prissy but with hesitation, lamenting, "I'd just come from a modern up-to-date integrated school in *What a Life*, and I couldn't understand why they'd want to bring back the 1800s. Most of my friends were progressive, going forward and looking forward. It was depressing for me."

Hattie McDaniel, the first Black actor to win an Oscar, said about her career playing racial stereotypes, "I rather play a maid than be one." But for McQueen, the dim-witted maid who gets slapped by the heroine in *Gone with the Wind*, this was not a role she would accept without protest.

When filming *Gone with the Wind*, Vivien Leigh, as Scarlett O'Hara, slapped Prissy too hard, and McQueen insisted that the slap be mimed in future takes.

When the NAACP discovered that McQueen was paid $200 a week to play the role of Prissy, far less than what was paid to white actors in *Gone with the Wind* (one of the highest-grossing films of all time), it boycotted the film.

McQueen voiced her objections when all the Black actors in *Gone with the Wind* were forced to travel in one car, while the white actors rode in limousines. She also joined a group of Black cast mates in protesting restroom segregation during the filming of the movie.

When the premiere of *Gone with the Wind* was held at a whites-only theater, McQueen was barred from attending. It wasn't until 1989, for the special fiftieth-anniversary viewing of *Gone with the Wind*, that McQueen was invited to attend and was honored.

Gone with the Wind began McQueen's lifelong rebellion against Hollywood racial stereotyping and discrimination, never wanting to play another part like Prissy but stereotyped to play the role of help. For the rest of her acting career, it would be difficult for McQueen to find roles. The roles she did accept were often uncredited, as in *Mildred Pierce*, *The Women* and *Affectionately Yours*.

In the 1940s, McQueen played Butterfly, Rochester's niece and Mary Livingstone's maid, in Jack Benny's radio program. In later years, people considered the role stereotypical and demeaning. According to McQueen, "You know, today they call me an Uncle Thomasina."

During World War II, McQueen appeared as a comedian on the Armed Forces Radio Service broadcast *Jubilee*. In 1947, after McQueen announced that "she would no longer accept 'handkerchief head' parts," she had only one movie offer for the next twenty years. "I had imagined that since I am an intelligent woman, I could play any kind of role." The industry wasn't ready to agree. In the early 1950s, McQueen turned to TV. In the show *Beulah*, she was typecast again, playing Beulah's best friend, another maid.

In 1979, McQueen starred in the after-school special *The Seven Witches of Joanna Peabody* as the fairy godmother. She earned an Emmy Award for Outstanding Individual Achievement in Children's Programming for her performance. Her final appearance was in the TV movie *Polly*, a remake of the *Pollyanna* story with a Black cast.

To quote McQueen, "I didn't mind playing a maid the first time because I thought that was how you got into the business. But after I did the same thing over and over, I resented it. I didn't mind being funny, but I didn't like being stupid." Proving that art doesn't imitate life, beginning in 1946 McQueen took classes at CCNY, UCLA, Southern Illinois, NYU and Queen's College. In 1975, at the age of sixty-four, she graduated from CCNY with a BA in political science.

When she wasn't acting, McQueen supported herself by working as a companion, a toy seller in Macy's, a cab dispatcher and a factory worker. In the mid-'60s, while supplementing her income as a waitress, she began a career in social work as a receptionist at a recreation center. To quote McQueen, "I didn't sit around and wait….If one is a worker, one can always find something to do."

McQueen was the victim of the most blatant kind of racial stereotyping when in 1979 she was passing through a Greyhound Bus terminal in Washington, D.C., and stopped to eat in the ladies' lounge. She was accosted by a security guard who mistook her for a pickpocket, was wrestled to the ground and sustained injury to several ribs. She filed a $300,000 lawsuit against Greyhound and was awarded $60,000 four years after the incident. She used the money to buy a small house in Augusta, Georgia, where she moved and gave music lessons, appeared on her own radio show, opened a restaurant and worked as a hostess at the most unlikely of venues, the Stone Mountain Memorial Museum of Confederate Times. Desiring anonymity, her neighbors knew her as Thelma McQueen, not Butterfly.

In 1995, Thelma "Butterfly" McQueen died at eighty-four from burns suffered from a heater accident in the house where she lived in Augusta, Georgia. As was her wish, McQueen's body was donated to science.

Of the role of Prissy, McQueen said, "I hated it. The part of Prissy was so backward. But now I'm very glad I made the film because I make a living off it. And you wouldn't be here if I hadn't been Prissy."

In McQueen's obituary, *Village Voice* contributor Michelle Wallace commented, "McQueen never got the work nor the credit she deserved." Her fight to get that work changed the stage for generations of Black actors to follow.

Chapter 7

SCIENCE AND TECHNOLOGY

Abraham Maslow

CCNY
Attended 1925–1927

Reflecting on his childhood, Abraham Maslow said, "It is a wonder I'm not psychotic!" This quote is from the man who is most well known for Maslow's hierarchy of needs, the top of the hierarchy only reached by the healthiest of people.

Born in 1908 in Brooklyn, New York, to immigrant parents, Abraham Maslow was the first of seven children. Like so many profiled in this book, he spent most of his childhood in the public library to escape a childhood of neglect or worse, as in Maslow's case. "My mother, a horrible woman, hated me utterly." She took his food and gave it to his siblings, attacked his physical appearance and punished any kindness he would show by destroying the object of his attention. As a result, at a young age Maslow developed such severe social anxiety that he could not enter a crowded subway. So great was this anxiety that it plagued him throughout his life. His father, often absent and an alcoholic, provided Maslow little comfort.

The only thing Maslow could credit his parents for was their emphasis on the need for education. Uneducated themselves, they saw the need for their children to attend school as the only way to rise above poverty.

Abraham Maslow.

Maslow attended Boys High School in the Bedford-Stuyvesant neighborhood of Brooklyn. The school was a college preparatory program with high academic standards. Alumni included Isaac Asimov, author; Emanuel Celler, U.S. congressman; Aaron Copland, composer and conductor; Norman Mailer, novelist; and Man Ray, artist.

In 1925, Maslow enrolled in CCNY. In 1926, in addition to his undergraduate curriculum and at the insistence of his parents, he began taking law courses at night. After realizing that he did not want to pursue a legal career, Maslow enrolled at Cornell University to study psychology. He dropped out of Cornell after one semester because of poor grades, the high cost of tuition and, surprisingly, a lack of interest in the subject that would become his life's work. Maslow returned to CCNY for a short time and eventually received a bachelor's degree, master's degree and PhD in psychology from the University of Wisconsin.

Explaining his circuitous educational path, he said, "I suddenly saw unrolling before me into the future the possibility of a science of psychology, a program of work which promised real progress, real advance, real solutions to real problems. All that was necessary was devotion and hard work."

Maslow's goal was always to obtain an academic appointment after receiving a PhD. Because of rampant anti-Semitism in the United States in the 1930s, this career path was thwarted. Instead, Maslow accepted a research fellowship at Columbia University. In 1938, at the end of this fellowship, with his ambitions still limited by prejudice, Maslow accepted a position at Brooklyn College, a predominantly Jewish institution. It was there that Maslow's research would turn the study of psychology upside down.

While many psychologists at the time were focused on studying the mentally ill, Maslow's interest focused on those who reached self-actualization by rising through what Maslow defined as a "hierarchy of needs."

In his 1943 paper, "A Theory of Human Motivation," Maslow defined this hierarchy of needs to include five levels: physiological needs (air, food, sleep and shelter); safety (employment, health); love (friendship, intimacy

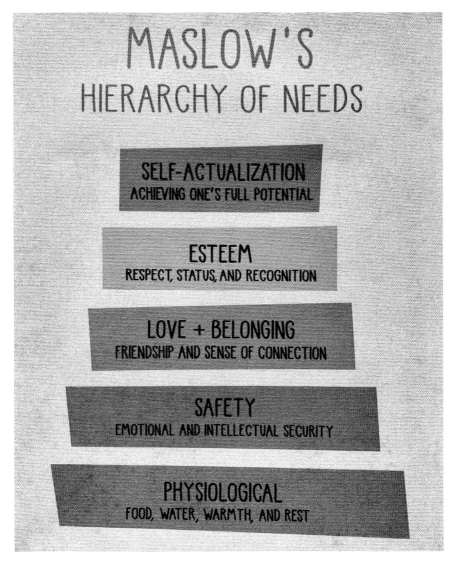

Abraham Maslow's famous hierarchy of needs, a key concept of his psychological theory based on fulfilling human needs in priority and improving self-actualization.

and family); esteem (respect, status and recognition); and, at the top of the triangle, self-actualization ("the full use and exploitation of talents, capacities and potentials"). Once one tier of needs is met and sustained, a person's focus would shift to the next tier.

While there were no pyramids in the original paper, Maslow's theory is usually illustrated as a pyramid. According to Douglas Kenrick, professor of psychology at Arizona State University, "The pyramid explains the longevity of Maslow's theory capturing a complicated idea in a very simple way."

Despite immediate criticism that his theory was neither grounded in empirical evidence nor effective in dealing with mental health issues, Maslow's hierarchy of needs continues to be taught in college psychology classes as the third school of psychology along with Freudian psychology and behaviorism. Today, Maslow is considered one of the most important and influential psychologists of the twentieth century.

Maslow's influence does not end with psychology. Maslow's hierarchy of needs has been adopted in the world of business management to identify the needs of staff beyond the paycheck. His influence on business management was best described by Gerard Hodgkinson, vice-dean at Alliance Manchester Business School: "One of the insights is that as managers we can shape the conditions that create people's aspirations."*

According to management expert and Maslow friend Warren Bennis, "Abe Maslow, a Jewish kid who really grew up poor, represented the American dream. All of his psychology really had to do with possibility, not restraints. His metaphysics were all about the possibilities of change, the possibilities of the human being to really fit into the democratic mode. The quality underlying all Maslow's thinking was his striking optimism about human nature and society."

Maslow died in 1970. At the time of his death, he was investigating the nature of evil in man.

Jonas Salk

CCNY
BS, 1934

In 1914, Jonas Salk was born in a tenement in East Harlem. Two plagues, the great influenza epidemic of 1918 in which 20 million people died worldwide and a major polio outbreak, tainted Salk's world before he was five. Salk would play a leading role in the eventual eradication of both.

Salk was the eldest of three sons of Daniel and Doris Salk, neither of whom had a formal education. His father was a garment worker who more

---

* As this profile is being written, railroad unions in the United States have rejected a proposed labor agreement guaranteeing a 24 percent increase in wages over three years because the union demands for quality-of-life benefits were not included in the agreement.

often than not found himself unemployed. His mother, a foreman in the garment industry before her marriage, was the primary family influence.

Salk had few fond memories of his childhood. His mother ruled his world, encouraging his intellectual growth and making certain that he learned to read at an early age. She told Jonas that he "had been born with a caul or special powers that he was destined for greatness. And he believed her." "As I look back on my beginnings," Salk said when interviewed in his later years, "I'm aware of the influence my family had on me, my parents especially, and the circumstances that existed in the world at that time."

At thirteen years old, after skipping several grades, Salk entered Townsend Harris High School, where he completed a four-year curriculum in three years. The school offered only token courses in physics, chemistry and biology. This suited Salk, since at thirteen he had little interest in science. According to Salk, "I was merely interested in things human."

Salk graduated from Townsend Harris and entered CCNY at fifteen years old, "a common age for freshman who had skipped multiple grades." Against his mother's wishes (she believed he was not sufficiently confrontational), Salk enrolled as a pre-law student. The first in his family to attend college, Salk only had to pay for books and streetcar fare. Tuition was free. And no one "got an advantage based on an accident of birth."

As a student at CCNY, he would face academic competition for the first time. At the end of his first semester at CCNY, Salk received a D in French; Cs in chemistry, math and English; and Bs in history and social studies. After receiving poor grades for the first time, and again against his mother's wishes, Salk decided to change his major from pre-law to pre-med. This time, Salk's mother told him that he was not physically strong enough to be a medical doctor and was better suited to teaching. But Salk's mother had taught her son that he was born with a caul, and Jonas Salk followed his caul.

In 1934, at the age of nineteen, Salk graduated from CCNY with a Bachelor of Science degree in chemistry, mediocre grades (an overall B average) and tacit Jewish quotas barring his admission to medical school. One thing did stand out on his medical school application: Salk did not want to practice medicine. "I didn't see myself practicing medicine," he said, as was the usual career for most medical school graduates. "I saw myself trying to bring science into medicine." With less than stellar credentials, Salk received his first and only letter of acceptance to medical school from Bellevue Hospital Medical College, soon to be renamed New York University College of Medicine. Tuition was "comparatively low, and the medical school did not discriminate against Jews."

Jonas Salk, developer of the first polio vaccine.

In addition to the money his parents borrowed to help him pay for tuition, Salk had a part-time job to help pay for books, a microscope and medical instruments, and he saved money by living at home. After his first year, scholarships and research fellowships covered the cost of medical school.

One of these fellowships was in a virus laboratory under the mentorship of Thomas Francis Jr., where Salk was introduced to a field that had never interested him but that would shape his life.

Thomas Francis Jr. gained recognition for discovering a new type of influenza virus. Salk wanted to test the hypothesis that one could kill a virus, destroying its infectivity, while retaining its ability to stimulate antibody production. According to Salk, "It was the laboratory work, in particular, that gave new direction to [my] life." By the time he left Francis's lab, Salk knew that a destroyed virus could impart immunity. In time, Salk and Francis would collaborate on some of the most important work of Salk's career.

Salk received his medical degree in 1939. He graduated Alpha Omega Alpha, the medical equivalent of Phi Beta Kappa, with "a desire to help humankind in general rather than single patients."

After medical school, Salk began his residency at Mount Sinai Hospital in New York, where he again worked in Thomas Francis's laboratory. In 1941, Salk accepted a National Research Council fellowship and in 1942 followed Dr. Francis to the University of Michigan, where the year before Francis had accepted the position of head of epidemiology. With Francis, Salk worked on behalf of the U.S. Army to develop commercial vaccines against the flu, work considered an important contribution to the war effort. By 1943, Salk and Francis had developed a virus vaccine effective against both type A and B influenza viruses. After little more than a decade, this work would lead Salk to the conquest of polio.

In an oral history, Salk recounted how his work with the polio vaccine came about. "After my internship, in '42, I went to Ann Arbor, Michigan. I was there until '47, then went on to Pittsburgh, to be somewhat independent of my mentor. The opportunity in Pittsburgh was something that others did not see, and I was advised against doing something as foolish as that because there was so little there. However, I did see that there was an opportunity to do two things. One was to continue the work I was doing on influenza, and two, to begin to work on polio. That was a very modest beginning." Salk immediately realized that the University of Pittsburgh School of Medicine lab was smaller than he had hoped, and he found the rules imposed by the university restrictive.

By 1948, Salk had gained the attention of Harry Weaver, the director of research at the National Foundation for Infantile Paralysis. Weaver offered Salk additional space, equipment and researchers to investigate polio. Salk later joined the National Foundation for Infantile Paralysis's polio project

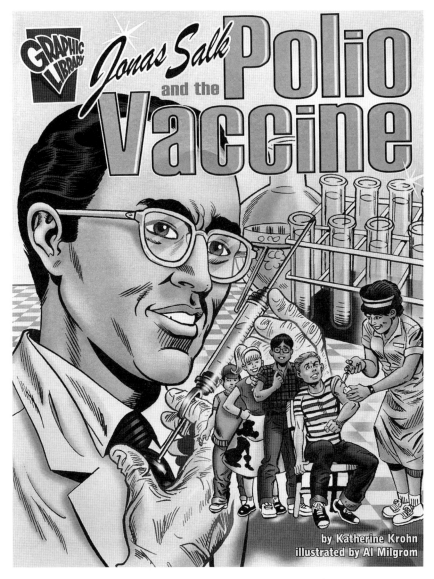

Graphic comic depicting the story of Jonas Salk and the polio vaccine.

established by President Franklin D. Roosevelt, himself a victim of polio. Eventually, almost all of the foundation's resources would go to support Salk's polio vaccine research efforts.

From the start, both Salk and his vaccine were controversial. Several eminent virologists insisted, up to the first field trial, that the killed virus vaccine should be withheld in favor of a live virus oral vaccine concurrently under development by Dr. Albert Sabin. Objections from one scientist prompted newscaster Walter Winchell to warn his radio audience not to take the vaccine because "it may be a killer." Salk, afraid that these scientists would try to derail his efforts, initially made and tested his vaccine in secret.

In 1952, Americans suffered the worst polio epidemic in history. By the time the outbreak ended, fifty-eight thousand people had been stricken. More than one-third were paralyzed, many of whom spent the rest of their lives in a wheelchair or bed. With this backdrop, Salk began

Jonas Salk on the cover of *Time* magazine.

testing his vaccine on children who had already been infected with the polio virus. His results indicated that the vaccine produced large amounts of the polio antibodies. The clinical trial was extended to include children who never had polio. In May 1952, Salk began preparations for a field trial in which more than 400,000 children were vaccinated. Salk vaccinated his own children in 1953.

Mass testing of the Salk polio vaccine began in April 1954, with the March of Dimes launching the biggest clinical trial in the history of medicine. The trial involved 1.5 million children between the ages of six and nine, each receiving a button that proclaimed them a "Polio Pioneer." Salk's vaccine was found to be 80 to 90 percent effective in preventing paralytic polio. By the end of the decade, the Salk vaccine would reduce the incidence of paralytic polio in the United States by 90 percent.

The news that the Salk vaccine was effective and safe caused what was labeled a "public sensation unequaled by any health development in modern times." The chairman of the Board of Directors of the American Medical Association, Dr. Dwight H. Murray, called it "one of the greatest events in the history of medicine." President Eisenhower praised Dr. Salk as a "benefactor of mankind." An opinion poll ranked Salk between Churchill and Gandhi as a revered figure of modern history.

The rebuke by the scientific community of Salk's work at the same time as his elevation to national hero was immediate and unrelenting. "As the heads of states around the world rushed to honor Salk, scientists—the one group whose adulation Salk craved—remained silent." Basil O'Connor, director of the National Foundation for Infantile Paralysis/March of Dimes, said, "They acted as if Salk had committed a felony. They accused Salk of failing to give proper credit to other researchers whose work had laid the foundation for his own." Salk, in fact, had tried to give them credit. But the media, not Salk, ignored the contributions of other scientists. According to *TIME* magazine, "This set the stage for difficulties throughout Salk's career wherein politics in and beyond the scientific community would override good science."

Wishing to escape the glare of the limelight, Salk retreated into his laboratory, but a tragic mishap served to keep the attention of the world's media focused on him. Two weeks after the announcement of the vaccine's discovery, eleven of the children who had received it developed polio. Altogether, about two hundred children developed paralytic polio; eleven died. All of the rogue vaccines originated from the same source, Cutter Laboratories in California. The vaccination campaign was halted by the surgeon general. It was found that Cutter Laboratories had used faulty batches of virus culture. After the adoption of standards that would prevent such a reoccurrence, vaccinations resumed. Over the course of the next two years, more than 200 million doses of Salk's polio vaccine were administered, without a single instance of vaccine-induced paralysis.

In 1961, a public health decision was made to replace the Salk vaccine with the vaccine developed by Albert Sabin, one of the virologists who had attempted to discredit Salk. Sabin's oral vaccine, made with a live virus, was cheaper and more convenient, but it was much riskier than the Salk vaccine. Salk would work the rest of his life to reverse this decision. Four years after Salk's death, in 1999, the Sabin vaccine was replaced with a new version of Salk's vaccine, which is still used today. Dr. Sabin, who died in 1993 at age eighty-six, continued to be infuriated at the mention of Dr. Salk. "It was pure kitchen chemistry," Dr. Sabin said of Salk's work. "Salk didn't discover anything." The millions of children saved from paralysis because of the Salk vaccine and their parents would disagree.

By 1969, not a single death from polio was reported in the United States, the first such year on record. When broadcast journalist Edward R. Murrow asked Salk who the owner was of the patent on the polio vaccine, Salk replied, "The people. There is no patent. Could you patent the sun?" If the Salk vaccine had been patented, it is calculated that it would be worth in excess of $7 billion today.

Jonas Salk official postage stamp, 2006.

With the opening of the Salk Institute for Biological Studies in 1963, Salk's dream to build a research complex for the investigation of biological phenomena was realized. His continuing research would lead to effective preventatives against a broad range of other infectious diseases, including measles, mumps and rubella. In later years, Salk also pioneered biomedical research on the immunological aspects of multiple sclerosis and cancer. By the mid-1980s, Salk had turned his attention to AIDS, attempting to develop an immunization that would prevent those already infected with HIV from developing AIDS. Unable to secure liability insurance for the project, the project was discontinued in 2007, twelve years after Salk's death in 1995 at eighty years of age.

Doris Salk predicted that her son Jonas was born with a caul. She was right. Over his lifetime, many honors would be conferred on Salk, including the Albert Lasker Award, the Robert Koch Medal, the Mellon Institute Award, a U.S. Presidential Citation and a Congressional Gold Medal. He was named a Chevalier de la Legion d'Honneur by the French government and was awarded honorary degrees from universities in the United States, Britain, Israel, Italy and the Philippines.

Two honors would elude Jonas Salk. As the result of scientific jealousy and latent anti-Semitism, Salk was never elected to the National Academy of Sciences of the United States. Nor did Salk receive a Nobel Prize for his work in creating the vaccine that eradicated polio from the face of the earth.

In 2006, the U.S. Postal Service, as part of the Distinguished Americans series, issued a postage stamp with his likeness to honor Jonas Salk. As part of the same series, a postage stamp was issued honoring Albert Sabin.

ROBERT AUMANN

CCNY
BS, 1950

Robert Aumann.

Robert Aumann was born in 1930 in Frankford am Main, Germany. His family line lived in Germany for centuries. When Robert Aumann was eight years old, his parents with their two sons left their homeland and their comfortable life and immigrated to New York. Their journey to America began two weeks before *Kristallnacht*. Leaving your ancestral homeland and all of your assets behind to go to a country where you knew no one and didn't speak the language seemed like an irrational act to the many Jewish families who believed that Adolf Hitler's policies were transitory. That decision saved the Aumann family from likely extermination. More than sixty-five years later, in Robert Aumann's 2005 Nobel Prize lecture "War and Peace," he offered this explanation for the seemingly irrational decisions: "A person's behavior is rational if it is in his best interests, given his information."

While Robert Aumann's parents gave up everything to come to America, they remained adamant that their sons would receive both a good Jewish and a good secular education. The first half year of the Aumann brothers' schooling was spent at PS 87 on the Upper West Side, considered one of the best public schools in the United States. Because there were no established Jewish schools in Manhattan at the time, the family moved to the Borough

137

Park neighborhood in Brooklyn so their sons could attend English- and Hebrew-speaking elementary schools and Rabbi Jacob Joseph Yeshiva Day School on the Lower East Side.

At the Yeshiva Day School, Robert Aumann met mathematics teacher Joseph "Joey" Gansler, and Aumann's interest in mathematics was born. Since the school had recently opened and class sizes were very small, Gansler gathered all the students around his desk, where they worked together on proofs, theorems and geometry. In an interview discussing his future mathematic success, Aumann stated, "All the credit goes to Joey Gansler."

Despite his blossoming interest in mathematics, Aumann debated whether he wanted to study secular subjects like mathematics or become a Talmudic scholar. So, he did both.

Aumann entered CCNY in 1946. When asked why he chose CCNY, Aumann answered:

> *Initially because it was free. My parents lost all their money in the move to America, since they were not allowed to take any capital out of Nazi Germany. My parents, my brother and I all worked. While at City College, I held down a job in a place that manufactured jewelry, running errands….*
>
> *I used to get up in the morning at 6:15, go to the university in uptown New York from Brooklyn—an hour and a quarter on the subway—then study calculus for an hour, then go back to the yeshiva on the lower east side for most of the morning then go back up to City College at 139th Street and study there until 10 pm. Then go home and do some homework or whatever and then I would get up again at 6:15. I did this for one semester, and then it became too much for me and I made the hard decision to quit the yeshiva and study mathematics at CCNY.*

It was decades later, when Aumann moved to Israel, that his interest in mathematics and the Talmud would intersect.

Aumann received his BS in mathematics from CCNY in 1950. He would be the second CCNY graduate of that decade to receive the Nobel Prize in economics, the other being Kenneth Arrow.

As an undergraduate at CCNY Aumann read about number theory, prime numbers and pure math. According to Aumann, "It was absolutely useless." But it was in vogue when Aumann entered graduate school at MIT, where Aumann completed his thesis in algebraic topology or knot theory. Fifty years later, Aumann found use for his work on knot theory when he helped his grandson study cancer caused by "knotted" DNA.

Aumann received his MS from MIT in 1952 and his PhD in mathematics in 1955. While at MIT, Aumann met John Nash. A few years later, their paths would cross again.

A year before receiving his PhD, Aumann took a job at Princeton University's Analytical Research Group. His assignment was to solve an urban air defense problem about defending a city from a squadron of aircrafts. The squadron consisted of many decoy planes, but a small percentage carried nuclear weapons. The problem was not going to be solved with the pure math Aumann had studied at MIT. The solution would come from game theory, a derivative of applied mathematics explained to Aumann and made famous by John Nash, Aumann's friend from MIT.

According to Aumann, "At the time it didn't interest me very much but when I was assigned the problem about decoys, I studied some game theory—just enough for this problem—and then the subject started attracting me in its own right." The encounter with Nash led Aumann to solve the problem of too many decoy planes and fostered an interest in applied mathematics that would define Aumann's career. Nash would become the subject of the 2001 movie *A Beautiful Mind*.

Game theory, the study of how and why people make decisions, is an approach used today in disciplines as diverse as economics, political science, international relations, law, business, public administration, evolutionary biology, computer science, conflict resolution and computer dating.* In 1964, game theory and its corollary of mutually assured destruction found its way into popular culture in the Hugo Award–winning movie *Dr. Strangelove or: How I Learned to Stop Worrying and Love the Bomb*.

In 1955, Aumann became a mathematics instructor at the Hebrew University of Jerusalem, fulling a wish that he and his brother had, to make a life in Jerusalem after the state of Israel was established in 1948. At the Hebrew University, he is best known for using game theory to analyze dilemmas in the Talmud. For example: What would you do if you were in Abraham's place and G-d directed you to kill your only son? In the context of game theory, if you are willing to take the challenge, you won't actually have to take it. It was Abraham's determination to kill Isaac that saved Isaac. In his pursuit to analyze Talmudic conflicts and dilemmas in terms of game

---

* This author was first introduced to applied mathematics and game theory in 1968 when War Games was a required course to receive a BA degree from the College of Liberal Arts at Temple University. This author used applied mathematics as the basis of her PhD dissertation and game theory in "real-life situations," including labor negotiations and courtroom and board room strategies.

theory, Aumann would achieve a goal that eluded him as a student at CCNY a decade earlier: to study secular subjects like mathematics and become a Talmudic scholar.

In 1991, Aumann founded the Center for the Study of Rationality at the Hebrew University to explore the rational basis of decision-making in a multidisciplinary setting. The pure math model that was the basis of Aumann's graduate thesis at MIT was formally usurped by the practical application of game theory.

Aumann holds six honorary doctorates and other awards, including the 2004 Israel Prize for Economic Research. Aumann won the 2005 Nobel Memorial Prize in Economic Sciences, which he shared with economist Thomas Schelling, for "having enhanced our understanding of conflict and cooperation through game theory analysis." The once outlier theory of applied mathematics is the underlying basis of all computer sciences.

Today, Aumann takes applied mathematics one step further in his belief that game theory can help us settle almost any real-life problem, whether it be matchmaking, the environment or the Israeli-Palestinian Conflict.

Chapter 8

FICTIONAL ALUMNI

The following fictional alumni (with the actors who personified them) all have four things in common: 1. The fictional alumni are all flawed; 2. The fictional alumni were the roles of a lifetime for the actors who played the parts; 3. Art or entertainment would imitate life for the fictional alumni and the actors who played the roles; and 4. The issues brought to the public's attention decades ago by the fictional alumni can be found on the front pages of today's newspapers.

GORDON GEKKO

(PLAYED BY MICHAEL DOUGLAS IN *WALL STREET*)

The movie *Wall Street* was released in 1987, and Michael Douglas's Gordon Gekko made "Greed Is Good" the mantra of Wall Street.

Unlike Michael Douglas, the privileged son of movie icon Kirk Douglas, Gordon Gekko was born on Long Island, the son of middle-class immigrants. Gekko's father was an electrical supplies salesman who died of a heart attack at age forty-nine with significant debts. Gekko was determined to succeed where his father failed.

Gekko attended the City College of New York, known at the time as the poor man's Harvard. A fictional contemporary at CCNY in 1963 recalled the twenty-one-year-old economics student as "ruthless, flamboyant, manipulative and above all greedy."

Rumors persisted that for his dissertation Gekko spent six months devising and operating a Ponzi scheme, persuading most of the student body to invest real money in a fictitious company. All the investors knew that the company did not exist. By the time the scheme imploded, Gekko was gone, without a degree from CCNY but with seed capital to begin building his fortune.

Gekko's first project was to sell an apartment complex for $800,000 before branching out into stock and bond trading. Eventually, he would make his fortune taking over underperforming businesses, which he restructured and sold for large

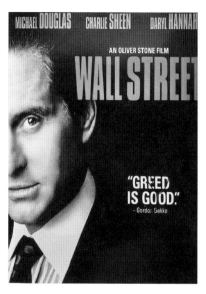

Michael Douglas as Gordon Gekko in Oliver Stone's *Wall Street*.

profits to the detriment of the employees of those companies who would lose not only their jobs but also their pensions. Never a nice guy, Gekko enjoyed defeating business leaders from Ivy League schools. He told his protégé, Bud Fox, in *Wall Street*, "Give me guys who are poor, smart, and hungry." Gekko described Ivy League MBAs as being "sheep who get slaughtered."

In a fictional 1985 speech at the University of California–Berkeley, School of Business Administration, Gekko said these iconic words: "The point is, ladies and gentlemen, that greed, for lack of a better word, is good. Greed is right. Greed works."

Gekko never lost sight of his origins or the fact that any respect that came his way had been earned and not inherited. When Gekko is complimented on his private club, he says, "Yeah not bad for a City College boy. I bought my way in now all these Ivy League schmucks are sucking my kneecaps."

When asked if Gordon Gekko was based on any individual, co-writers Oliver Stone and Stanley Weiser responded, "Gekko is a composite based on several real-world financiers, but he is a mostly fictitious character that takes inspiration from real life." The film's producer Ed Pressman added that one of the inspirations for Gordon Gekko was Michael Milken. Milken was arrested in 1989 and convicted of multiple counts of fraud and racketeering.

Despite the fact that Gordon Gekko was a villain in *Wall Street*, many in finance saw him as a tragic hero. In 2010, amid a global financial crisis,

Douglas reprised the role of Gordon Gekko in *Wall Street: Money Never Sleeps.* Michael Douglas, concerned that people would see Gekko as a role model, worked with the FBI to create a documentary exposing insider trading. In 2012, the FBI released a public service announcement video of Douglas calling on viewers to report financial crimes.

For his portrayal of Gordon Gekko in the original film *Wall Street*, Michael Douglas won an Academy Award for Best Actor in 1988. In 2003, the American Film Institute named Gekko no. 24 of the top 100 film villains. In 2005, the American Film Institute also named his quote about greed no. 57 of the top 100 film quotes. In 2008, Gekko was named the fourth-richest fictional character by *Forbes*, which estimated his wealth at $8.5 million.

Gordon Gekko remains a movie legend. The lessons learned with the rise and fall on screen of Gordon Gekko would be quickly overshadowed by the 2008 arrest of Bernard Madoff, the fall of FTX's Sam Bankman-Fried and the most recent implosion of Silicon Valley bank SVB.

LENNIE BRISCOE

(PLAYED BY JERRY ORBACH ON *LAW AND ORDER*)

The character of Lennie Briscoe was based on a similar NYPD character portrayed by Jerry Orbach in 1981 in the film *Prince of the City*. Briscoe would be the third-longest-serving main cast member on the TV series *Law & Order*. As Lennie Briscoe, his role would bring worldwide fame to Jerry Orbach.

Briscoe was born in 1940. Like Orbach, Briscoe's father was a Jewish immigrant, and his mother was Roman Catholic. Briscoe attended CCNY before joining the NYPD.

The cases Briscoe investigated between 1992 and 2004 were often based on real cases and recent headlines about corrupt police officers, corrupt city officials and bureaucrats and hate crimes against religious and minority communities.

Jerry Orbach took the role so seriously that he appeared in a 2001 demonstration in which police officers demanded higher wages from Mayor Giuliani's administration. "All I can do is try and represent you guys on a TV screen and make you look as good as I can," Orbach was quoted as saying in *Newsday*. "I could never go out and not know if I'm coming home that night the way you do."

His portrayal of Lennie Briscoe resulted in Orbach's nomination for a 2000 Primetime Emmy Award for Outstanding Lead Actor in a Drama Series. (He lost to James Gandolfini for *The Sopranos*.) The TV series *Law & Order* won the 1997 Primetime Emmy for Outstanding Drama Series. *TV Guide* named Lennie Briscoe one of the top twenty-five greatest television detectives of all time.

In 2002, Orbach was named a "Living Landmark" by the New York Landmarks Conservancy. He quipped that the honor meant "that they can't tear me down."

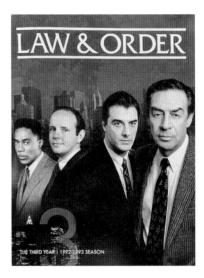

Jerry Orbach as Lennie Briscoe (*far right*) in *Law & Order*.

Briscoe, like Orbach, died in 2004.

In 2005, Orbach was posthumously awarded a Screen Actors Guild Award for Outstanding Performance by a Male Actor in a Drama Series for his role as Lennie Briscoe on *Law & Order*.

The day after Orbach's death, the marquees on Broadway were dimmed. This is one of the highest honors of the American theater world.

TOBY ZIEGLER

(PLAYED BY RICHARD SCHIFF ON *THE WEST WING*)

The West Wing ran from 1999 to 2006, winning seven Emmy Awards, including Outstanding Special Class Program in 2002. Richard Schiff won an Emmy for Outstanding Supporting Actor in a Drama Series for his portrayal of Toby Ziegler, White House communications director.

Toby Ziegler was born in 1954. Ziegler's father worked for Murder Incorporated, the Jewish Mafia's enforcement arm. With art (in this case television) imitating life, Richard Schiff's paternal grandfather was associated with the New York mob of Meyer Lansky and Bugsy Siegel. This would not be the only similarity between Richard Schiff and the fictional character Toby Ziegler.

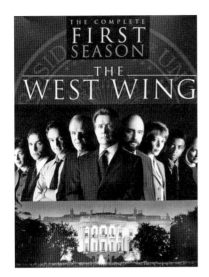

Richard Schiff as Toby Ziegler (*fourth from the right, right of center*) in Aaron Sorkin's *The West Wing*.

Both Ziegler and Schiff grew up in New York City. Ziegler and Schiff attended CCNY. Ziegler graduated. Schiff dropped out of high school and obtained an equivalency diploma. Schiff entered CCNY in 1973 but again dropped out of school after not showing up for finals. He returned to New York in 1975 to study acting at CCNY. CCNY would grant Schiff an honorary Doctor of Humane Letters degree. He also received the Townsend Harris Medal from CCNY for Outstanding Post-Graduate Achievement. Past recipients include Upton Sinclair, Paddy Chayefsky, Edward G. Robinson and Jonas Salk.[*]

Ziegler's jobs after college all involve political campaigns for New York candidates until his last campaign as communications director for the Bartlet for America presidential campaign. According to Ziegler, he never won a campaign until this one.[†] He would work for seven years as the White House communications director under President Bartlet, learning later that he had not been the president's first choice.

Despite his more privileged upbringing, Schiff's early jobs before acting were less than glamorous. They included driving a taxi in New York City and cleaning buses in the Greyhound terminal on 11th Avenue. Schiff was cast in the role of Toby Ziegler, an unhappy man, over many other actors. Toby Ziegler became the role for which Schiff is best known.

The West Wing was about an American presidency and staffers in the West Wing who addressed the problems of the day, including energy, tax cuts and terrorism—problems replicated in the headlines of today. Schiff recalled, "Because of *The West Wing*, I think I have a voice."

The final season of *West Wing* involved a storyline around a leak of classified information, which the *New York Times* compared to the real-life leak investigation of the Valerie Plame affair. But the *West Wing* leak story had been developed sixteen months before the Plame affair. The *West Wing*

---

[*] Richard Schiff's father dropped out of CCNY, where he had been studying business, to get a bachelor's and law degrees in an accelerated program at Brooklyn Law School in the late 1940s. He was inspired to return to CCNY to receive his degree after his son received an honorary doctorate.

[†] A *Wall Street Journal* poll in 2016 named Martin Sheen's Josiah Bartlet as the second-greatest fictional president, behind Harrison Ford's President James Marshall in *Air Force Once*.

plot involves an unauthorized disclosure about a secret military space shuttle and the investigation to find the source of the leak. The source was assumed to be Toby Ziegler. Ziegler confessed (to protect the real leaker), and the U.S. Attorney threated to indict him. The last act of President Bartlet while in office was to pardon Ziegler. In real Washington, D.C., the grand jury indicted I. Lewis "Scooter" Libby, Vice President Dick Cheney's chief of staff, on charges of obstruction of justice, perjury and making false statements in the course of the real-life Plame investigation. President Trump fully pardoned Libby.

DON DRAPER

(PLAYED BY JON HAMM ON *MAD MEN*)

Creator Matthew Weiner initially thought that Jon Hamm was "too handsome" for the role of Don Draper in *Mad Men*, a television series set in a fictional 1960s Madison Avenue advertising agency. When Weiner discovered that Hamm had suffered the early loss of his parents, similar to Draper's backstory, the rest became advertising and TV history. *Mad Men* debuted on July 19, 2007, with almost 1.4 million viewers.

Don Draper, the lead character in *Mad Men*, is a "suave, married, philandering executive with an obscure past. Born Richard Whitman, the son of an alcoholic, he grew up in a brothel in Philadelphia. A sickly child, he was nursed back to health by a prostitute who then raped him. As a private during the Korean War, he would assume the identity of a lieutenant who he accidently killed. It was at that moment Whitman saw a chance to leave behind his family, his childhood and his name." He took it, assuming the identity of Don Draper, the man he had killed.

The reimagined Don Draper moved to New York, where he found work as a salesman and copywriter. After a few years, he would become Sterling Cooper's creative director, where he would save the agency from ruin more than once. In the end, Draper would cost Sterling Cooper a lucrative military contract because he feared that the background check required of him would expose his real identity. When asked about his education, Draper responded, "I strung together several non-consecutive years while attending City College of New York at night." Richard Whitman didn't graduate high school.

Jon Hamm as Don Draper in AMC's *Mad Men*.

Off screen, Jon Hamm's childhood and youth were a perfect backdrop for the role that would make him famous. Hamm's parents divorced when he was two, and he lived with his mother until she died when he was ten; he then moved in with his father and grandmother. Hamm says that he used memories of his father to portray Draper, describing his father as an "influential man of business and society hiding great inner turmoil." While a member of Upsilon Chapter of Sigma Nu fraternity at the University of Texas, Hamm was arrested for participating in a violent hazing incident. He made a plea deal, completing probation under the terms of a deferred adjudication, allowing him to avoid being convicted of a crime. Charges were dismissed in 1995 following the completion of probation.

In 2007, Hamm was chosen to play Don Draper from more than eighty candidates. This was his breakthrough role. Hamm won a Golden Globe Award for Best Actor in a Television Series–Drama in 2008 and 2016, followed by a Primetime Emmy Award for Outstanding Lead Actor in 2015 and two Screen Actors Guild Awards.

In 2009, *Ask Men* named the fictional Don Draper the most influential man in the world ahead of real-life figures. Comcast listed Draper among TV's Most Intriguing Characters. In 2010, *Entertainment Weekly* included Draper on its list of the 100 Greatest Characters of the Last 20 Years. And in 2015 it named Draper one of the 25 Best TV Characters of the Past 25 Years.

Don Draper would not be the last fabulist to gain media and public attention. In the last twelve months, Elizabeth Holmes of Theranos fame and collapse and Sam Bankman-Fried of crypto exchange FTX collapse come to mind. Perhaps the person who most closely resembles Don Draper, aka Richard Whitman, is recently elected Congressman George Santos.

BACKSTORY

The Ephebic Oath, an oath of civic responsibility, is affirmed by graduating students of CCNY at every commencement. The Oath speaks to what it means to be CCNY Made:

> *We who are graduating from The City College of New York, do this day, after the manner of the Athenian youths of old about to enter public life take this oath of devotion to the City of New York: we will never bring disgrace to our city by any act of dishonesty or cowardice nor ever desert our suffering comrades in the ranks; we will fight for the ideals and sacred things of the city, both alone and with many; we will revere and obey the city's laws and do our best to incite alike respect and reverence in those about us who are prone to annul them and set them at naught; we will strive unceasingly to quicken the public's sense of civic duty; and thus, in all these ways, we will strive to transmit this city not only not less, but greater, better and more beautiful than it was transmitted to us.*

APPENDIX

Bess Myerson

Hunter College
BA, 1945

Bess Myerson, the first and only Jewish Miss America, faced rejection before she was crowned until her ignominious departure from public service. Today, she is remembered for her fall from grace, but between her reign and her fall, Bess Myerson led two New York City agencies, Consumer Affairs and Cultural Affairs; advised three U.S. presidents; and accomplished more to improve the lives of consumers than any other Miss America since the pageant's start in 1921.

Myerson was born in the Bronx on July 16, 1924, the second of three daughters, to Louis and Bella Myerson, immigrants from Russia. A brother, Joseph, died of diphtheria at age three. Her father supported the family by working as a housepainter and handy man. The family lived in the Sholem Aleichem Cooperative, a project housing 250 Jewish working-class families.

In 1937, Myerson entered the second class of the High School of Music and Art as a music major, studying piano and the flute. She graduated from Hunter College in 1945 with honors and a degree in music, fulfilling her mother's wish that her daughters be well versed in music. According to Myerson, her "mother's desire was not based upon an appreciation of music

Bess Myerson on the cover of *LIFE* magazine, 1971.

but because she wanted an insurance policy for her daughters so they could support themselves as teachers if they ever became widows."

Notwithstanding her mother's motives, Myerson had her own ambition. She was determined to earn a graduate degree from Juilliard or Columbia, buy her own Steinway piano and become a concert pianist. To support her ambition, she gave piano lessons for fifty cents per hour—that is, until her sister Sylvia came up with a better idea.

According to Myerson, without her knowledge her sister entered her photograph in the 1945 Miss New York City contest. Myerson won the contest and subsequently became a contestant in the Miss America pageant, the first year the pageant offered the winner a $5,000 college scholarship.

Myerson won the bathing suit contest wearing a borrowed suit that her sister had to stretch to fit Myerson's five-foot-ten frame. She also won the talent contest, playing George Gershwin's "Summertime" on the flute and excerpts from Grieg's Concerto on the piano. Her mother's insurance policy paid off, although not like she had imagined.

Myerson became the first postwar Miss America, the first Miss New York to be crowned Miss America, the first Miss America to be awarded a pageant scholarship and the first (and only) Jewish Miss America. It was the last first that had the greatest impact on her life.

In 1945, the atrocities of World War II defined what it meant to be Jewish. Myerson's crowning represented the acceptance of Jews in America. That acceptance would be short-lived and illusory.

Myerson, raised in a tightknit Jewish community, was unprepared for the blatant anti-Semitism she would face as a Miss America pageant contestant and winner. Even before the competition began, a pageant director told her that she would have a better chance of winning if she changed her last name to something more "attractive" like Marshall, code for a less obviously Jewish name. Susan Dworkin in the book *Miss America, 1945: Bess Myerson's Own Story* described Myerson's decision to ignore that advice as one of the most important she ever made.

During her reign as Miss America, Myerson faced continuing anti-Semitism, as evidenced when three of the five sponsoring companies of the pageant withdrew their support from her post-pageant tour. Businesses refused to offer her sponsorships, as was customary for pageant winners. She was denied entrance to hotels. And when an invitation to speak at a country club was revoked because she was Jewish, Myerson cut her Miss America tour short by six months. Subsequently, she agreed to a six-month lecture tour for the Anti-Defamation League of B'nai B'rith, speaking out against prejudice with a speech titled "You Can't Be Beautiful and Hate." While on this tour, Myerson was discovered by a television producer, and her career as a TV personality was born.

For eight years, Myerson was the pretty face that launched game shows and pitched products on television. Then she joined the team of *I've Got a Secret*, and for the next nine years she was recognized as a TV staple in homes around the United States.

In 1969, with Myerson's recognition as a TV personality well established, Mayor John Lindsay named Myerson New York City's first commissioner of Consumer Affairs, where she proved that she was not just a pretty face. As commissioner of Consumer Affairs, Myerson issued the first city regulation in the nation requiring retailers to post unit prices on products to make comparison shopping easier. She endeared herself to New Yorkers by criticizing manufacturers for putting too many peanuts in jars labeled "mixed nuts" and restaurants that sold hamburgers that were less than 100 percent beef. She set up a consumer hotline and a consumer action team and called for clearer dating labels for perishable foods, all the while recovering $5 million for defrauded consumers. In 1971, she graced the cover of *LIFE* magazine with the headline "A Consumer's Best Friend."

Bess Meyerson (*right*) with Jackie Onassis in front of Grand Central Station.

During the 1960s and '70s, Myerson expanded her political profile, winning presidential appointments to boards focused on crime and violence under Lyndon Johnson, world hunger and mental health under Jimmy Carter and workplace issues under Gerald Ford. In 1975, she joined a group of prominent New Yorkers, including Jackie Kennedy Onassis, to prevent Grand Central Terminal from being destroyed.

In 1974, while considering running for the U.S. Senate, Myerson was diagnosed with ovarian cancer. After a year and a half of radiation and chemotherapy, she returned to work. Almost a decade later, she would suffer a brain aneurysm and again fully recover, ultimately returning to work.

In 1977, Myerson chaired Ed Koch's campaign for mayor of New York City. Seen by his side throughout the campaign, she is credited with winning the election for him. In return, Koch backed Myerson as a candidate in the 1980 Democratic primary for the U.S. Senate. She lost the primary to Elizabeth Holtzman. In 1982 Koch appointed Myerson commissioner of the Department of Cultural Affairs. But the seeds of her fall from grace had already been planted.

In 1980, Myerson met Carl "Andy" Capasso. By 1983, he was under investigation by Rudolph Giuliani, then the U.S. Attorney in Manhattan, regarding a $53.6 million sewage contract that Capasso obtained not long after Myerson became Cultural Affairs commissioner. Myerson was not implicated in the award of this contract, but her reputation and career would be forever tarnished when Capasso's wife filed for divorce.

Myerson was dubbed the "Bess Mess" by the press after Hortense Gabel, the presiding justice in Capasso's divorce proceedings, reduced his ex-wife's support payments and it was revealed that Myerson had given Gabel's unemployed daughter, Sukhreet, a job as an assistant. Mayor Koch, Myerson's friend, called for a grand jury investigation. Myerson was indicted along with Hortense Gabel and Capasso, accused of mail fraud, conspiracy, obstruction of justice and violating bribery laws. Myerson refused to testify, pleading that it would be self-incrimination.

To add insult to injury and more headlines, Sukhreet was the chief witness against the defendants in the case including her mother, Hortense Gabel, and Myerson. The jury acquitted the three defendants of all charges. Capasso pleaded guilty to unrelated federal income tax evasion charges and was sentenced to prison. In April 1987, Myerson was forced to resign her position as commissioner of Cultural Affairs.

After decades of public service, Myerson would forever be remembered not for her beauty nor for her good works but for the salacious headlines that ended her reign as one of the most influential people in New York City. Myerson turned away from the spotlight that had followed her since she was crowned Miss America and dedicated the rest of her life to Jewish charities. She became the national commissioner of the Anti-Defamation League. In 1998, she endowed the ADL's annual Bess Myerson Campus Journalism Award. Always seeing herself as a Jewish public servant, Myerson became the spokeswoman for Israeli Bonds and pledged $1.1 million for the construction of the Museum of Jewish History in Battery Park.

When asked whether she would enter the Miss America Pageant again knowing how it all ended, her answer was a mixed message. Sitting next to a "nice Jewish man" at a dinner party, she was heard to say, "I should have married someone like you at twenty-four and moved to Scarsdale." At other times, she reminisced, "Being the same girl from the Bronx that I was then. Having a great desire to be a concert pianist and not having the money to buy a big black Steinway? I sure would."

Myerson died in her California home on December 14, 2014, at ninety years of age. Her obituary in the *New York Times* read, "Her [Myerson's] death which occurred in the relative obscurity in which she lived her last years, had not been publicly announced but was confirmed by public records."

Despite her dramatic fall from the spotlight, there's one thing New Yorkers of a certain age will agree on: there will never be another Bess Myerson.

NYC INDEPENDENT BUDGET OFFICE

THĒ **DREYFUS**
CORPORATION

PHILIP L. TOIA
VICE PRESIDENT

June 25th, 1990

To: The Honorable Elizabeth Holtzman, Comptroller
     The Honorable Andrew Stein, City Council President
     The Honorable Fernando Ferrer, Borough President
     The Honorable Peter Vallone, Speaker, City Council

     The Independent Budget Office Advisory Board is pleased
to recommend three candidates for the position of Director,
Independent Budget Office.

     The candidates are listed in the order in which they
were ranked by the Advisory Board. They are:

     1. Ronny Jane Goldsmith, Ph.D.
     2. Hugh O'Neill, Ph.D.
     3. Joel D. Platt

     Resumes for each of the candidates are attached.

     The three candidates are all well qualified for the
position, in our opinion, and each can bring a unique quality to
the task of building a new office for the City of New York.

     Over one hundred fifty individuals expressed an interest
in the position and submitted a resume. Those resumes were
reviewed by the total Advisory Board and were rated by each
member.

MANAGERS OF THE DREYFUS GROUP OF MUTUAL INVESTMENT FUNDS
200 PARK AVENUE, NEW YORK, N.Y. 10166/TELEPHONE: 922-6000/DOM TELEX: 148373/INT'L TELEX, 620393/CABLE: DRYFUND NEW YORK

-2-

Candidates who were rated as qualified by at least three Advisory Board members were reviewed by a sub-committee of the Board and the list was narrowed to six individuals who were invited to interview. An interviewing committee of four Board members conducted the interviews and discussed the results with the Board. The candidates being recommended represent the consensus opinion of the Board.

We are satisfied that either of the candidates can do the job and that they represent a diversity of talent and background such that the selecting committee can go forward with a strong choice for the first Director of the Independent Budget Office.

Sincerely,

Philip L. Toia
Chairman, IBO Advisory Board

PLT:pac

Magazine Covers and U.S. Postage Stamps

BIBLIOGRAPHY

Alfred Stieglitz

Artsmia. "Get the Picture: Abbott and Stieglitz." 2022. http://artsmia.org/get-the-picture/abbott/compare_stieglitz.html.

Belden-Adams, Kris. "Stieglitz, the Steerage (Article)." Khan Academy, 2014. https://www.khanacademy.org/humanities/ap-art-history/later-europe-and-americas/modernity-ap/a/stieglitz-the-steerage.

Hostetler, Lisa. "Alfred Stieglitz (1864–1946) and American Photography." The MET, 2004. https://www.metmuseum.org/toah/hd/stgp/hd_stgp.htm.

William Klein

Barcio, Phillip. "IdeelArt: The Online Gallerist." Ideel Art, March 17, 2017. https://www.ideelart.com/magazine/william-klein.

Contessa Gallery. "William Klein: Biography." 2022. https://www.contessagallery.com/artist/William_Klein/biography.

Maher, James. "Many Lives—the History and Photography of William Klein." James Maher Photography, April 15, 2022. https://jamesmaherphotography.com/street_photography/many-lives-the-photography-of-william-klein.

Robert, McFadden D. "William Klein, Who Photographed the Energy of City Life, Dies at 96." New York Times, September 12, 2022. https://www.nytimes.com/2022/09/12/arts/william-klein-dead.html.

World Photography Organization. "William Klein to Receive Outstanding Contribution to Photography Award." 2012. https://web.archive.org/web/20121029003105/http:/www.worldphoto.org/news-and-events/william-klein-to-receive-outstanding-contribution-to-photography-award.

Garry Winograd

Brody, Richard. "How Garry Winogrand Transformed Street Photography." *The New Yorker*, September 15, 2018. https://www.newyorker.com/culture/photo-booth/how-garry-winogrand-transformed-street-photography.

Grundberg, Andy. "Garry Winogrand, Innovator in Photography." *New York Times*, March 21, 1984, sec. B. https://www.nytimes.com/1984/03/21/obituaries/garry-winogrand-innovator-in-photography.html.

———. "Perfecting the Medium, c. 1900–c. 1945." Encyclopædia Britannica, 2022. https://www.britannica.com/technology/photography/Perfecting-the-medium-c-1900-c-1945.

International Center of Photography. "Garry Winogrand." May 17, 2016. https://www.icp.org/browse/archive/constituents/garry-winogrand?all%2Fall%2Fall%2Fall%2F0.

Public Delivery. "Garry Winogrand's Women Are Beautiful—50 Years Later." July 8, 2022. https://publicdelivery.org/garry-winogrand-women-are-beautiful.

Zhou, Dennis. "Mass Media's Martyr: Reassessing Garry Winogrand." ARTnews, October 2, 2018. https://www.artnews.com/art-in-america/features/mass-medias-martyr-reassessing-garry-winogrand-60131.

Ben Shahn

Archives of American Art, Smithsonian Institution. Oral history interview with Ben Shahn, April 14, 1964.

———. Oral history interview with Ben Shahn, September 27, 1968.

The Art Story Foundation. "Ben Shahn Artworks & Famous Paintings." 2021. https://www.theartstory.org/artist/shahn-ben/artworks.

———. "Ben Shahn Paintings, Bio, Ideas." 2021. https://www.theartstory.org/artist/shahn-ben.

Biography. "Ben Shahn." https://biography.yourdictionary.com/ben-shahn.

Edwards, Susan H. "Ben Shahn's New Deal: The Resettlement Administration (RA) and the Farm Security Administration (FSA)." Harvard Art Museums, September 1999. https://web.archive.org/web/20080509005855/http://www.artmuseums.harvard.edu/shahn/servlet/webpublisher.WebCommunication?ia=tr&ic=pt&t=xhtml&x=edwards.

Encyclopædia Britannica. "Ben Shahn." March 10, 2021.

J. Weekly. "Did Bernie Sanders Take His Cues from Ben Shahn." December 29, 2016. https://www.jweekly.com/2016/06/03/did-bernie-sanders-take-his-cues-from-ben-shahn.

Linden, Diana L. "An Essay about Artist Ben Shahn." Jonathan Boos, June 8, 2020. https://jonathanboos.com/ben-shahn-1940.

Marquette University. "Ben Shahn: For the Sake of a Single Verse." 2019. https://www.marquette.edu/haggerty-museum/ben-shahn.php.

Mintie, Katherine. "Art and Politics in the 1940s: Ben Shahn." Harvard Art Museums, April 22, 2020. https://harvardartmuseums.org/article/art-and-politics-in-the-1940s-ben-shahn.

Montgomery Museum of Fine Arts. "Ben Shahn." 2020. https://collection.mmfa.org/artist-maker/info/131.

Museum of Modern Art. "Ben Shahn. Handball. 1939: MoMA." 2021. https://www.moma.org/collection/works/33365.

New York Times. "Ben Shahn, Artist, Is Dead Here at 70; Ben Shahn, Painter Who Espoused Social Causes, Dies." March 15, 1969.

Sartle. "Ben Shahn." March 21, 2021. https://www.sartle.com/artist/ben-shahn.

Shahn, Ben. Interview with Edwin Rosskam. Rutgers University Library Special Collections, January 10–14, 1965. https://www.state.nj.us/state/historykids/pdfs/immigration/ben_shahn.pdf.

Smithsonian American Art Museum. "Ben Shahn." https://americanart.si.edu/artist/ben-shahn-4384.

WikiArt. "Ben Shahn—102 Artworks—Painting." https://www.wikiart.org/en/ben-shahn.

Ralph Lauren

CNN. "Ralph Lauren Fast Facts." September 20, 2020. https://www.cnn.com/2015/01/30/us/ralph-lauren-fast-facts/index.html.

———. "Ralph Lauren Upset by Biography." March 21, 2003. http://edition.cnn.com/2003/WORLD/europe/03/21/design360.ralph.lauren.reut.

Elkins, Kathleen. "From Dirt Poor to a $7 Billion Fortune—the Incredible Rags-to-Riches Story of Ralph Lauren." *Business Insider*, May 4, 2015. https://www.businessinsider.com/how-ralph-lauren-went-from-dirt-poor-to-a-multi-billionaire-2015-5.

Forbes. "Ralph Lauren." 2021. https://www.forbes.com/profile/ralph-lauren/?sh=fa86b473d0c4.

Fury, Alexander. "Ralph Lauren: The Patriarch of Fashion's Rise from Rag-Trader to American Royalty." *Independent*, September 30, 2015. https://www.independent.co.uk/life-style/fashion/features/ralph-lauren-patriarch-fashion-s-rise-rag-trader-american-royalty-a6674416.html.

Grant, Nick, and Jian Deleon. "50 Things You Didn't Know About Ralph Lauren." Complex Networks, October 1, 2015. https://www.complex.com/style/2015/10/things-you-didnt-know-about-ralph-lauren/ralph-lauren-first-investor-norman-hilton.

Green, David B. "Ralph Lauren Is Born, Will Build an Empire Based on Cary Grant Fantasy." Haaretz, October 14, 2015. https://www.haaretz.com/jewish/premium-an-admirer-of-cary-grant-is-born-1.5408440.

Gross, Michael. "Genuine Authentic: The Real Life of Ralph Lauren." March 5, 2016. https://mgross.com/writing/books/genuine-authentic.

———. *Genuine Authentic: The Real Life of Ralph Lauren.* New York: William Morrow, an imprint of HarperCollins Publishers, 2018.

HELLO! Fashion. "The Fascinating Rags to Riches Story of Fashion Mogul Ralph Lauren." November 6, 2012. https://web.archive.org/web/20180628015912/

https:/fashion.hellomagazine.com/fashion-news/20121106960/ralph-lauren-rags-to-riches.

Luecke, Andrew D. "How Ralph Lauren Sold the American Dream." *Esquire*, October 14, 2014. https://www.esquire.com/style/mens-fashion/a23767/how-ralph-lauren-sold-the-american-dream.

May, Shelia. "Smithsonian's Star-Spangled Banner to Undergo Three-Year Conservation." National Museum of American History, Smithsonian Institution, June 29, 2015. https://Americanhistory.si.edu/Press/Releases/Smithsonians-Star-Spangled-Banner-Undergo-Three-Year-Conservation.

NICHE. "Fashion Legend Ralph Lauren." 2013. https://www.nichemagazine.ca/legends-icons/fashion-legend-ralph-lauren.

Oprah. "Oprah Talks to Ralph Lauren." October 15, 2002. https://www.oprah.com/omagazine/oprah-interviews-ralph-lauren/1?print=1.

Saner, Emine. "'It's Not About Fabric, It's About Dreams': How Ralph Lauren Created an Empire." *Guardian*, October 2, 2015. https://www.theguardian.com/fashion/2015/oct/02/its-not-about-fabric-its-about-dreams-how-ralph-lauren-created-an-empire.

Tschorn, Adam. "Ralph Lauren: 5 Things You Should Know About HBO's New Designer Documentary." *Los Angeles Times*, November 12, 2019. https://www.latimes.com/lifestyle/story/2019-11-12/ralph-lauren-hbo-documentary.

Jean Nidetch

Biography. "Jean Nidetch." 2000. https://biography.yourdictionary.com/jean-nidetch.

Branson-Potts, Hailey. "Jean Nidetch Dies at 91; a Founder of Weight Watchers." *Los Angeles Times*, April 30, 2015. https://www.latimes.com/local/obituaries/la-me-jean-nidetch-20150430-story.html.

Horatio Alger Association. "Honoring Perseverance, Integrity and Excellence." 2022. https://horatioalger.org/members/member-detail/jean-nidetch.

Horwell, Veronica. "Jean Nidetch Obituary." *Guardian*, May 1, 2015. https://www.theguardian.com/lifeandstyle/2015/may/01/jean-nidetch.

Knight, Kathryn. "Jean Nidetch Made a Fortune from Weightwatchers—but a New Book Reveals How She Gambled Money Away." *Daily Mail*, June 12, 2020. https://www.dailymail.co.uk/news/article-8412249/Jean-Nidetch-fortune-WeightWatchers-new-book-reveals-gambled-money-away.html.

McFadden, Robert D. "Jean Nidetch, a Founder of Weight Watchers, Dies at 91." *New York Times*, April 29, 2015. https://www.nytimes.com/2015/04/30/business/jean-nidetch-dies-at-91-co-founder-of-weight-watchers-and-dynamic-speaker.html.

Meltzer, Marisa. "Why I Worship the Weight Watchers Founder Jean Nidetch." *New York Times*, May 6, 2017. https://www.nytimes.com/2017/05/06/fashion/who-founded-weight-watchers.html.

Public Broadcasting Service. "Who Made America? | Innovators | Jean Nidetch."
  2004. https://www.pbs.org/wgbh/theymadeamerica/whomade/nidetch_
  hi.html.
Rosenblit, Rachel. "Weight Watchers Founder Jean Nidetch Was a 'Well-
  Fluencer' Long Before Those Existed." *Washington Post*, April 15, 2020.
  https://www.washingtonpost.com/entertainment/books/weight-watchers-
  founder-jean-nidetch-was-a-well-fluencer-long-before-those-existed-one-
  writer-is-giving-the-trailblazer-her-due/2020/04/15/1ba5fa9c-7f19-11ea-
  a3ee-13e1ae0a3571_story.html.
Sedensky, Matt. "A Former Housewife, Weight Watchers Founder Jean Nidetch
  Dies at 91." *Times of Israel*, May 4, 2015. https://www.timesofisrael.com/a-
  former-housewife-weight-watchers-founder-jean-nidetch-dies-at-91.

Stanley Kaplan

Arenson, Karen W. "Stanley Kaplan, Pioneer in Preparing Students for
  Exams, Dies at 90." *New York Times*, August 25, 2009. https://www.nytimes.
  com/2009/08/25/education/25kaplan.html.
Kaplan, Stanley H., and Anne Farris. *Stanley H. Kaplan, Test Pilot: How I Broke Testing
  Barriers for Millions of Students and Caused a Sonic Boom in the Business of Education.*
  New York: Simon & Schuster, 2001.
McDougall, Sophia. "The Story of Stanley Kaplan." Kaplan Pathways,
  August 13, 2018. https://www.kaplanpathways.com/blog/the-story-of-
  stanley-kaplan.
Sullivan, Patricia. "Test-Prep Pioneer Stanley H. Kaplan Dies at 90."
  Washington Post, August 25, 2009. https://www.washingtonpost.com/wp-
  dyn/content/article/2009/08/24/AR2009082402105.html.
Wong, Carina. "Stanley H. Kaplan, Founder of the Test Preparation Industry,
  Dies at 90." Kaplan, August 22, 2009. https://kaplan.com/about/press-
  media/stanley-h-kaplan-founder-of-the-test-preparation-industry-dies-at-90.

Andrew Grove

BBC News. "Former Intel Chief Andrew Grove Dies Aged 79." March 22, 2016.
  https://www.bbc.com/news/technology-35221693.
CUNY Newswire. "Intel's Grove Gives $26 Million to CCNY's School
  of Engineering." October 28, 2005. https://web.archive.org/
  web/20161002120129/http://www1.cuny.edu/mu/forum/2005/10/28/
  intels-grove-gives-26-million-to-ccnys-school-of-engineering.
Gaither, Chris. "Technology: Andy Grove's Tale of His Boyhood in
  Wartime." *New York Times*, November 12, 2001, sec. C. https://www.nytimes.
  com/2001/11/12/business/technology-andy-grove-s-tale-of-his-boyhood-in-
  wartime.html.

Goldstein, Ken. "The Many Lessons of Andy Grove." Good Men Project, April 26, 2016. https://goodmenproject.com/business-ethics-2/many-lessons-andy-grove-gmp.

Heinz Awards. "Andrew Grove." http://www.heinzawards.net/recipients/andrew-grove.

Intel Newsroom. "Andrew S. Grove 1936–2016." March 27, 2019. https://newsroom.intel.com/news-releases/andrew-s-grove-1936-2016/#gs.5m1l6x.

Kandell, Jonathan. "Andrew S. Grove Dies at 79; Intel Chief Spurred Semiconductor Revolution." *New York Times*, March 21, 2016. https://www.nytimes.com/2016/03/22/technology/andrew-grove-intel-obituary.html.

Langeneckert, S. "Andrew S. Grove." Encyclopædia Britannica. https://www.britannica.com/biography/Andrew-S-Grove.

Ramo, Joshua Cooper. "Andrew Grove: A Survivor's Tale." *TIME*, December 29, 1997. http://content.time.com/time/subscriber/article/0,33009,987588-7,00.html.

Rivett-Carnac, Mark. "The True Story of Intel Pioneer Andrew Grove, *TIME*'s 1997 Man of the Year." *TIME*, March 22, 2016. https://time.com/4267150/andrew-grove-intel-survivor-biography-budapest.

Sager, Mike. "Andy Grove: What I've Learned." *Esquire*, January 29, 2007. https://www.esquire.com/entertainment/interviews/a1449/learned-andy-grove-0500.

Abraham Beame

Beame, Abraham D. "Abraham D. Beame, Oral History Interview—RFK—6/27/1978." By Roberta W. Greene. Robert F. Kennedy Oral History Program of the Kennedy Library, June 27, 1978, 1–14.

Doyle, Dennis. "About Abraham D. Beame." Richmond Hill Historical Society. https://web.archive.org/web/20010803145113/http://richmondhillhistory.org/abeame.html.

Encyclopaedia Judaica. "Beame, Abraham David." November 29, 2022. https://www.encyclopedia.com/religion/encyclopedias-almanacs-transcripts-and-maps/beame-abraham-david.

Martinez, Isadora. "New York City History." LaGuardia & Wagner Archives, 2021. https://www.laguardiawagnerarchive.lagcc.cuny.edu.

McFadden, Robert D. "Abraham Beame Is Dead at 94; Mayor during 70s Fiscal Crisis." *New York Times*, February 11, 2001. https://www.nytimes.com/2001/02/11/nyregion/abraham-beame-is-dead-at-94-mayor-during-70-s-fiscal-crisis.html.

Washington Post. "New York Mayor Abraham Beame." February 11, 2001. https://www.washingtonpost.com/archive/local/2001/02/11/new-york-mayor-abraham-beame/b1c74218-709e-4677-a0bc-352e5f9c879f.

Ed Koch

American Archive of Public Broadcasting. "American Experience: Stonewall Uprising; Interview with Edward Koch, 1 of 2." WGBH (GBH and the Library of Congress), Boston, MA, and Washington, D.C. http://americanarchive.org/catalog/cpb-aacip-15-52w3sqwm.

Encyclopædia Britannica. "Ed Koch." December 8, 2022. https://www.britannica.com/biography/Ed-Koch.

Flegenheimer, Matt, and Rosa Goldensohn. "The Secrets Ed Koch Carried." *New York Times*, May 7, 2022. https://www.nytimes.com/2022/05/07/nyregion/ed-koch-gay-secrets.html.

Goldensohn, Rosa, and Matt Flegenheimer. "The Story of Former Mayor Ed Koch's Life in the Closet: The Brian Lehrer Show." WNYC, May 12, 2022. https://www.wnyc.org/story/story-former-mayor-ed-kochs-life-closet.

McFadden, Robert D. "Edward I. Koch, a Mayor as Brash, Shrewd and Colorful as the City He Led, Dies at 88." *New York Times*, February 1, 2013. https://www.nytimes.com/2013/02/02/nyregion/edward-i-koch-ex-mayor-of-new-york-dies.html.

Notable New Yorkers. "Edward I Koch." Columbia University Libraries, 2006. http://www.columbia.edu/cu/lweb/digital/collections/nny/koche/profile.html.

Schwartzman, Paul. "Ed Koch, Outspoken Former Mayor of New York, Dead at 88." *Washington Post*, February 1, 2013. https://www.washingtonpost.com/local/obituaries/ed-koch-outspoken-former-mayor-of-new-york-dead-at-88/2013/02/01/451d6c18-c9e4-11e1-aea8-34e2e47d1571_story.html.

Eric Adams

Ax, Joseph. "Eric Adams Poised to Be New York's Next Mayor." Reuters, July 7, 2021. https://www.reuters.com/world/us/new-results-expected-new-york-citys-democratic-mayoral-race-2021-07-06.

Barkan, Ross. "The 'Shocking' and Unpredictable Political Journey of Eric Adams." Gothamist, February 6, 2020. https://gothamist.com/news/eric-adams-borough-president-brooklyn-mayor.

Flegenheimer, Matt, Michael Rothfeld and Jeffery C. Mays. "What Kind of Mayor Might Eric Adams Be? No One Seems to Know." *New York Times*, October 23, 2021. https://www.nytimes.com/2021/10/23/nyregion/eric-adams-mayor-nyc.html.

New York City Office of the Mayor. "Mayor's Bio: City of New York." 2022. https://www.nyc.gov/office-of-the-mayor/bio.page.

New York State Senate. "Senator Eric Adams." July 13, 2015. https://www.nysenate.gov/senators/eric-adams/bio.

Rodriguez, Matos. "NYC's New Mayor Attended Queensborough." Queensborough Community College, November 3, 2021. https://www.qcc.cuny.edu/news/2021/11/Mayor.html.

Williams, Juan. "Eric Adams Is Making White Liberals Squirm." *The Atlantic*, September 23, 2021. https://www.theatlantic.com/ideas/archive/2021/08/eric-adams-police-new-york/619869.

Felix Frankfurter

American-Israeli Cooperative Enterprise. "Felix Frankfurter." 2021. https://www.jewishvirtuallibrary.org/felix-frankfurter.

Belpedio, James R. "Felix Frankfurter." Free Speech Center, 2009. https://www.mtsu.edu/first-amendment/article/1330/felix-frankfurter.

Fox, John. "The Supreme Court. Expanding Civil Rights. Biographies of the Robes. Felix Frankfurter: PBS." Educational Broadcasting Corporation, December 2006. https://www.thirteen.org/wnet/supremecourt/rights/robes_frankfurter.html.

Harvard Crimson. "Felix Frankfurter Dies; Retired Judge Was 82." February 23, 1965. https://www.thecrimson.com/article/1965/2/23/felix-frankfurter-dies-retired-judge-was.

Hirsch, H.N. *Enigma of Felix Frankfurter*. New Orleans, LA: Quid Pro Books, 2014.

Hohenstein, Kurt. "Chasing the Devil Around the Stump: Securities Regulation, the SEC and the Courts." Securities and Exchange Commission Historical Society, 2021. http://www.sechistorical.org/museum/galleries/ctd/ctd_04c_minds_frankfurter.php.

Jones, David M. "Felix Frankfurter." Immigration to the United States, 2015. https://immigrationtounitedstates.org/508-felix-frankfurter.html.

Mason, Alpheus Thomas. "Felix Frankfurter Reminisces." *Annals of the American Academy* 333, no. 1 (January 1, 1961): 182–84. https://doi.org/https://doi.org/10.1177/000271626133300149.

New World Encyclopedia. "Felix Frankfurter." April 5, 2017. https://www.newworldencyclopedia.org/entry/Felix_Frankfurter.

Simkin, John. "Felix Frankfurter." Spartacus Educational, January 2020. https://spartacus-educational.com/USAfrankfurter.htm.

Tames, George. "Felix Frankfurter Is Dead; Influenced the Law Widely; Felix Frankfurter, Member of the Supreme Court for 23 Years, Dies in Capital at 82." *New York Times*, February 23, 1965.

Twitter, Ian Millhiser. "*Brown v. Board of Education* Came Very Close to Being a Dark Day in American History." ThinkProgress, May 15, 2015. https://archive.thinkprogress.org/brown-v-board-of-education-came-very-close-to-being-a-dark-day-in-american-history-dd231ad0f2f2.

Urofsky, Melvin I. "The Failure of Felix Frankfurter." *University of Richmond Law Review* 26, no. 1 (1991): 175–212. https://core.ac.uk/download/pdf/232780944.pdf.

Yardley, Jonathan. "On Dupont Circle: Franklin and Eleanor Roosevelt and the Progressives Who Shaped Our World." *Washington Post*, August 10, 2012. https://www.washingtonpost.com/opinion/on-dupont-circle-franklin-and-eleanor-roosevelt-and-the-progressives-who-shaped-our-world-by-james-srodes/2012/08/10/780ca3fc-da4a-11e1-a3f5-b4e7667a8298_story.html.

Benjamin Ferencz

Benjamin B. Ferencz. "Biography." March 10, 2020. https://benferencz.org/biography.

Ferencz, Benjamin. Interview with Joan Ringelheim. *USHMM*, August 24, 1994. https://collections.ushmm.org/search/catalog/irn507286.

———. *Parting Words: 9 Lessons for a Remarkable Life*. London: Sphere, 2021.

Finkelstein, Daniel. "Parting Words: Nine Lessons for a Remarkable Life by Benjamin Ferencz Review—What You Know When You're 100." *Sunday Times*, December 26, 2020. https://www.thetimes.co.uk/article/parting-words-nine-lessons-for-a-remarkable-life-by-benjamin-ferencz-review-what-you-know-when-youre-100-vbk5tmnr7?region=global.

Heller, Karen. "The Improbable Story of the Man Who Won History's 'Biggest Murder Trial' at Nuremberg." *Washington Post*, August 31, 2016. https://www.washingtonpost.com/lifestyle/style/the-last-surviving-nuremberg-prosecutor-has-one-ultimate-dream/2016/08/31/3b1607e6-6b95-11e6-ba32-5a4bf5aad4fa_story.html.

Kenigsberg, Ben. "'Prosecuting Evil' Review: At 98, His Passion for Justice Hasn't Dimmed." *New York Times*, February 21, 2019. https://www.nytimes.com/2019/02/21/movies/prosecuting-evil-review.html.

Stahl, Lesley. "What the Last Nuremberg Prosecutor Alive Wants the World to Know." CBS News, June 27, 2021. https://www.cbsnews.com/news/nuremberg-prosecutor-ben-ferencz-60-minutes-2021-06-27.

Weinke, Annette. "Benjamin Ferencz." Geschichte Menschenrechte, December 2, 2013. https://www.geschichte-menschenrechte.de/personen/benjamin-ferencz.

Wiener, Tom. "'War's End': World War II Veterans Project Sponsors Anniversary Symposium." Library of Congress Information Bulletin, June 28, 2012. https://web.archive.org/web/20120628011658/http://www.loc.gov/loc/lcib/0506-8/vhp.html.

Henry Kissinger

Bilefsky, Dan. "Kissinger Suggests that Ukraine Give up Territory to Russia, Drawing a Backlash." *New York Times*, May 24, 2022. https://www.nytimes.com/2022/05/25/world/europe/henry-kissinger-ukraine-russia-davos.html.

Biography. "Henry Kissinger." A&E Networks Television, April 2, 2014. https://www.biography.com/political-figure/henry-kissinger.

Clarke, Paul. "Deutsche Bank Hires Henry Kissinger and Former Chair Achleitner for New Advisory Board." Financial News, November 1, 2022. https://www.fnlondon.com/articles/deutsche-bank-hires-henry-kissinger-and-former-chair-achleitner-for-new-advisory-board-20221101.

Draper, Theodore. "Little Heinz and Big Henry." *New York Times*, September 6, 1992. https://archive.nytimes.com/www.nytimes.com/books/98/12/06/specials/isaacson-kissinger.html?_r=1&oref%3B=slogin.

Encyclopædia Britannica. "Henry Kissinger." August 20, 2022. https://www. britannica.com/biography/Henry-Kissinger.

Hagan, Joe. "The Once and Future Kissinger." *New York Magazine* (April 11, 2019). https://nymag.com/news/people/24750.

Kaplan, Fred. "Henry Kissinger Wrote a Peace Plan for Ukraine. It's Ludicrous." *Slate*, December 16, 2022. https://slate.com/news-and-politics/2022/12/ henry-kissinger-ukraine-peace-plan-vladimir-putin.html.

Kissinger, Henry. "How to Avoid Another World War." *The Spectator*, December 14, 2022. https://www.spectator.co.uk/article/the-push-for-peace.

Schwartz, Thomas A. "The Making of Henry Kissinger." History Reader, September 9, 2020. https://www.thehistoryreader.com/us-history/the-making-of-henry-kissinger.

Simkin, John. "Henry Kissinger." Spartacus Educational, 2020. https://spartacus-educational.com/COLDkissinger.htm.

Wall Street Journal. "Henry Kissinger Is Worried about 'Disequilibrium.'" August 13, 2022. https://www.wsj.com/articles/henry-kissinger-is-worried-about-disequilibrium-11660325251?st=7oqyd4cmhairzx2&reflink=share_ mobilewebshare.

White, Jeremy B., Sam Sutton, Carly Sitrin, Bill Mahoney and Josh Gerstein. "Henry Kissinger: Good or Evil?" *Politico* (October 10, 2015). https://www. politico.com/magazine/story/2015/10/henry-kissinger-history-legacy-213237.

WWD. "Henry Kissinger in the Swinging Seventies." June 4, 2013. https://wwd. com/fashion-news/fashion-features/celebrating-henry-kissinger-6967416.

Colin Powell

DeYoung, Karen. *Soldier: The Life of Colin Powell*. N.p.: Vintage, 2007.

National Public Radio. "'It Worked for ME': Life Lessons from Colin Powell." May 22, 2012. https://www.npr.org/2012/05/22/153296714/it-worked-for-me-life-lessons-from-colin-powellhttps://www.npr.org/2012/05/22/153296714/ it-worked-for-me-life-lessons-from-colin-powell.

Powell, Colin L., and Joseph E. Persico. *My American Journey*. New York: Ballantine Books, 2003.

Powell, Colin L., and Tony Koltz. *It Worked for Me: In Life and Leadership*. New York: Harper Perennial, 2014.

Schwab, Nikki. "Colin Powell: Bad Student." *Washington Examiner*, May 30, 2012. https://www.washingtonexaminer.com/colin-powell-bad-student.

Upton Sinclair

Coodley, Lauren. "Upton Sinclair." Encyclopædia Britannica. https://www. britannica.com/biography/Upton-Sinclair.

Greenspan, Jesse. "7 Things You May Not Know About 'The Jungle.'" History, January 19, 2016. https://www.history.com/news/7-things-you-may-not-know-about-the-jungle.

Historical Society of Southern California. "Upton Sinclair." 2009. https://web.archive.org/web/20120527075221/http://www.socalhistory.org/bios/upton_sinclair.html.

Lohnes, Kate. "The Jungle." Encyclopædia Britannica. https://www.britannica.com/topic/The-Jungle-novel-by-Sinclair.

Novak, Matt. "How Upton Sinclair Turned The Jungle Into a Failed New Jersey Utopia." Gizmodo, August 8, 2013. https://gizmodo.com/how-upton-sinclair-turned-the-jungle-into-a-failed-new-1015213490.

Press in America. "Upton Sinclair." December 8, 2008. http://pressinamerica.pbworks.com/w/page/18360241/Upton%20Sinclair.

Public Broadcasting Service, American Experience. "How 'The Jungle' Changed American Food." YouTube, 2020. https://youtu.be/OuukM9OY-is.

Rouse, K.L. "Meat Inspection Act of 1906." Encyclopædia Britannica, June 23, 2020. https://www.britannica.com/topic/Meat-Inspection-Act.

Sinclair, Upton. *The Jungle*. Project Gutenberg, 1906. https://www.gutenberg.org/files/140/140-h/140-h.htm.

———. "What Life Means to Me." *The Cosmopolitan* 41 (May 1906).

Slotnik, Daniel E. "Upton Sinclair, Whose Muckraking Changed the Meat Industry." *New York Times*, June 30, 2016. https://www.nytimes.com/interactive/projects/cp/obituaries/archives/upton-sinclair-meat-industry.

U.S. House of Representatives. "The Pure Food and Drug Act." https://history.house.gov/Historical-Highlights/1901-1950/Pure-Food-and-Drug-Act.

Unti, Bernard. "The Jungle: Upton Sinclair's Roar Is Even Louder to Animal Advocates Today." Humane Society of the United States, March 10, 2006. https://web.archive.org/web/20100106223608/http://www.hsus.org/farm/news/ournews/the_jungle_roar.html.

Whitman, Alden. "Upton Sinclair, Author, Dead; Crusader for Social Justice, 90; 90 Books, Including 'Oil!' and 'The Jungle,' Caused Many to Join His Protests." *New York Times*, November 26, 1968. https://www.nytimes.com/1968/11/26/archives/upton-sinclair-author-dead-crusader-for-social-justice-90-90-books.html.

Paddy Chayefsky

Campbell, Colin. "Paddy Chayefsky Dead at 58; Playwright Won Three Oscars." *New York Times*, August 2, 1981, sec. 1. https://www.nytimes.com/1981/08/02/obituaries/paddy-chayefsky-dead-at-58-playwright-won-three-oscars.html?auth=linked-google1tap.

Chronopoulos, Themis. "Paddy Chayefsky's 'Marty' and Its Significance to the Social History of Arthur Avenue, The Bronx, in the 1950s." *Bronx County Historical Society Journal* 44 (2007): 50–59. https://cronfa.swan.ac.uk/Record/cronfa30486.

Considine, Shaun. *Mad as Hell: The Life and Work of Paddy Chayefsky*. Lincoln, NE: iUniverse.com, 2000.

Dwyer, Shawn. "Paddy Chayefsky." Turner Classic Movies, 2021. https://www. tcm.com/tcmdb/person/32855%7C120222/Paddy-Chayefsky/#biography.

Encyclopedia. "Marty." November 25, 2021. https://www.encyclopedia.com/ arts/educational-magazines/marty.

Encyclopædia Britannica. "Paddy Chayefsky." July 28, 2021. https://www. britannica.com/biography/Paddy-Chayefsky.

Hubbard, Lauren. "Who Was Bob Fosse's Close Friend Paddy Chayefsky?" *Town & Country*, April 24, 2019. https://www.townandcountrymag.com/leisure/ arts-and-culture/a27180293/paddy-chayefsky-fosse-verdon-facts.

Itzkoff, David. "Notes of a Screenwriter, Mad as Hell." *New York Times*, May 19, 2011. https://www.nytimes.com/2011/05/22/movies/paddy-chayefskys-notes-for-network-film.html?referringSource=articleShare.

Jacobson, Jay. "Marty, 1955." *Jay's Classic Movie Blog*, November 16, 2021. https:// www.jaysclassicmovieblog.com/post/marty-1955.

JewAge. "Paddy Chayefsky—Biography." 2008. https://www.jewage.org/wiki/ru/ Article:Paddy_Chayefsky_-_Biography.

Myers, Scott. "How They Write a Script: Paddy Chayefsky." Medium, November 19, 2018. https://gointothestory.blcklst.com/how-they-write-a-script-paddy-chayefsky-2912eee0e9f7.

Palmer, Landon. "'Network' Turns 40: Here Are 3 Ways It Changed How We Understand News Media." IndieWire, December 1, 2016. https://www.indiewire. com/2016/12/network-anniversary-news-media-1201750526.

Teeman, Tim. "Paddy Chayefsky: The Dark Prophet of 'Network' News." Daily Beast, July 12, 2017. https://www.thedailybeast.com/paddy-chayefsky-the-dark-prophet-of-network-news?ref=scroll.

Mario Puzo

Chilton, Martin. "Mario Puzo at 100: The Godfather Author Never Met a Real Gangster, but His Mafia Melodrama Remains Timeless." *Independent*, October 15, 2020. https://www.independent.co.uk/arts-entertainment/films/features/ mario-puzo-at-100-the-godfather-author-never-met-a-real-gangster-but-his-mafia-melodrama-remains-timeless-b863424.html.

City College of New York. "Why Humanities and the Arts?" March 2, 2021. https://www.ccny.cuny.edu/humanities/why-humanities-and-arts.

Course Hero. "The Godfather Author Biography." 2021. https://www.coursehero. com/lit/The-Godfather/author.

Gussow, Mel. "Mario Puzo, Author Who Made 'The Godfather' a World Addiction, Is Dead at 78." *New York Times*, July 3, 1999, sec. B. https://www. nytimes.com/1999/07/03/movies/mario-puzo-author-who-made-the-godfather-a-world-addiction-is-dead-at-78.html.

Homberger, Eric. "Mario Puzo: The Author of the Godfather, the Book the Mafia Loved." *Guardian*, July 4, 1999. https://www.theguardian.com/news/1999/jul/05/guardianobituaries.

Joudeh, J. "The Godfather." Encyclopædia Britannica, March 16, 2017. https://www.britannica.com/topic/The-Godfather-novel-by-Puzo.

Moore, M.J. *Mario Puzo: An American Writer's Quest*. New York: Heliotrope Books, 2019.

Official Mario Puzo Library. "The Dark Arena." 2019. http://www.mariopuzo.com/dark_arena/dark_arena.shtml.

———. "The Fortunate Pilgrim." 2019. http://www.mariopuzo.com/fortunate_pilgrim/fortunate_pilgrim.shtml.

———. "The Godfather." 2019. http://www.mariopuzo.com/godfather/godfather.shtml.

———. "Mario Puzo Biography." http://www.mariopuzo.com/biography.shtml.

———. "Mario Puzo: The Godfather Papers and Other Confessions." 2019. http://www.mariopuzo.com/gf_papers/gf_papers.shtml.

Paglia, Camille. "It All Comes Back to Family." *New York Times*, May 8, 1997, sec. B. https://www.nytimes.com/1997/05/08/garden/it-all-comes-back-to-family.html.

Soft Schools. "Mario Puzo Facts." 2005. https://www.softschools.com/facts/authors/mario_puzo_facts/1434.

Tucker, Reed. "How Mario Puzo Penned 'The Godfather' to Get Out of Debt—and Made Bank." *New York Post*, March 2, 2019. https://nypost.com/2019/03/02/how-mario-puzo-penned-the-godfather-to-get-out-of-debt-and-made-bank.

Ira Gershwin

Ardoin, John. "The Great American Songbook—Mr. Music and Mr. Words." Public Broadcasting Service, July 31, 2014. https://www.pbs.org/wnet/gperf/the-great-american-songbook-mr-music-and-mr-words/141.

Encyclopædia Britannica. "Ira Gershwin." December 2, 2021. https://www.britannica.com/biography/Ira-Gershwin.

Gershwin. "The Gershwin Brothers." 2022. http://gershwin.com/the-gershwin-brothers.

———. "Ira Gershwin." 2022. http://gershwin.com/ira.

Larkin, Colin, ed. "Ira Gershwin." Public Broadcasting Service, October 2, 2012. https://www.pbs.org/wnet/broadway/stars/ira-gershwin.

National Public Radio. "Michael Feinstein: What I Learned from the Gershwins." October 13, 2012. https://www.npr.org/2012/10/13/162738387/michael-feinstein-what-i-learned-from-the-gershwins.

New York Times. "Widow of Ira Gershwin Endows Literacy Center." March 25, 1987, sec. C. https://www.nytimes.com/1987/03/25/arts/widow-of-ira-gershwin-endows-literacy-center.html.

Songwriters Hall of Fame. "Ira Gershwin." 2022. https://www.songhall.org/profile/Ira_Gershwin.

Summers, Kim. "Ira Gershwin Biography, Songs, & Albums." AllMusic, 2022. https://www.allmusic.com/artist/ira-gershwin-mn0000200301/biography.

Wilson, John S. "Ira Gershwin, Lyricist, Dies; Songs Embodied Broadway." *New York Times*, August 18, 1983, sec. A. https://www.nytimes.com/1983/08/18/obituaries/ira-gershwin-lyricist-dies-songs-embodied-broadway.html.

Edgar Yipsel Harburg

Donaldson, Leigh. "Yip Harburg: Father of the Socially Conscious Lyric." American Songwriter, October 11, 2019. https://americansongwriter.com/yip-harburg-father-of-the-socially-conscious-lyric.

Goodman, Amy. "A Tribute to Yip Harburg: The Man Who Put the Rainbow in the Wizard of Oz." Democracy Now!, November 25, 2004. https://web.archive.org/web/20071114223630/http://www.democracynow.org/article.pl?sid=04%2F11%2F25%2F0832252.

Lorenz, Kathleen Phillis. "'Something Sort of Grandish'—Spotlight on E.Y. 'Yip' Harburg." 42nd Street Moon, 2003. https://web.archive.org/web/20120207112034/http://www.42ndstmoon.com/History/Harburg.html.

Public Broadcasting Service. "E.Y. 'Yip' Harburg." October 15, 2012. https://www.pbs.org/wnet/broadway/stars/e-y-yip-harburg.

Wilson, John S. "E.Y. Harburg, Lyricist, Killed in Car Crash." *New York Times*, March 7, 1981, sec. 1. https://www.nytimes.com/1981/03/07/obituaries/ey-harburg-lyricist-killed-in-car-crash.html.

Yip Harburg. "Biography." https://yipharburg.com/about-yip-2/biography.

————. "Stage Musicals & Motion Pictures." https://yipharburg.com/resources/stage-screen.

YouTube. "A Tribute to Blacklisted Lyricist Yip Harburg: The Man Who Put the Rainbow in The Wizard of Oz." 2017. https://www.youtube.com/watch?v=PkwYBfx5f9Y.

Zollo, Paul. "Yip Harburg: The Man Who Brought the Rainbow to the Wizard of Oz." American Songwriter, January 20, 2020. https://americansongwriter.com/somehwere-over-the-rainbow-wizard-of-oz-behind-the-song.

Frank Loesser

Encyclopædia Britannica. "Frank Loesser." June 25, 2022. https://www.britannica.com/biography/Frank-Loesser.

Frank Loesser. "Bio." May 26, 2019. https://frankloesser.com/bio.

Gross, Terry. "Celebrating Frank Loesser with Michael Feinstein." Fresh Air Archive: Interviews with Terry Gross, February 25, 2011. https://freshairarchive.org/segments/celebrating-frank-loesser-michael-feinstein.

Harris, Kathryn. "Frank and Family." Music Theatre International, January 27, 2017. https://www.mtishows.com/news/frank-and-family.

Kennedy Center. "Frank Loesser." 2022. https://www.kennedy-center.org/artists/l/lo-lz/frank-loesser.

Loudon, Christopher. "Frank Loesser: A Most Talented Fella." JazzTimes, April 26, 2019. https://jazztimes.com/features/columns/frank-loesser-a-most-talented-fella.

McDonell-Parry, Amelia. "'Baby, It's Cold Outside': A Brief History of the Holiday Song Controversy." *Rolling Stone*, December 11, 2020. https://www.rollingstone.com/feature/baby-its-cold-outside-controversy-holiday-song-history-768183.

Music Theatre International. "Frank Loesser." 2022. https://www.mtishows.com/people/frank-loesser.

Official Masterworks Broadway. "Frank Loesser." February 25, 2015. https://masterworksbroadway.com/artist/frank-loesser.

Partridge, Kenneth. "The Complicated, Controversial History of 'Baby, It's Cold Outside.'" Mental Floss, December 15, 2021. https://www.mentalfloss.com/article/653345/baby-its-cold-outside-song-music-controversy.

Russaw, Jeanine Marie. "Why 'Baby, It's Cold Outside' Remains Controversial and Recently Got a Revamp from John Legend." *Newsweek*, December 6, 2019. https://www.newsweek.com/why-baby-its-cold-outside-remains-controversial-recently-got-revamp-john-legend-1475792.

Shout, John D. "Frank Loesser." Public Broadcasting Service, October 2, 2012. https://www.pbs.org/wnet/broadway/stars/frank-loesser.

Songwriters Hall of Fame. "Frank Loesser." 2022. https://www.songhall.org/profile/Frank_Loesser.

Edward G. Robinson

Encyclopædia Britannica. "Edward G. Robinson." September 7, 2022. https://www.britannica.com/biography/Edward-G-Robinson.

JewAge. "Edward G. Robinson—Biography." 2022. https://www.jewage.org/wiki/ru/Article:Edward_G._Robinson_-_Biography.

Shannon. "Edward G. Robinson: The Screen's Cultured Gangster." Vanguard of Hollywood, September 28, 2022. https://vanguardofhollywood.com/star-of-the-month-edward-g-robinson.

Siegel, Scott, and Barbara Siegel. "Edward G. Robinson." Film Noir 'Net, Eric B. Olsen, 2022. https://bernardschopen.tripod.com/egrobin.html.

Turner Classic Movies. "Edward G. Robinson." 2022. https://prod-www.tcm.com/tcmdb/person/163201%7C45179/Edward-G.-Robinson#biography.

Whitman, Alden. "Edward G. Robinson, 79, Dies; His 'Little Caesar' Set a Style." *New York Times*, January 27, 1973. https://www.nytimes.com/1973/01/27/archives/edward-g-robinson-79-dies-his-little-caesar-set-a-style-man-of.html.

Zero Mostel

Aurthur, Robert Alan. "Hanging Out with Zero Mostel." *Esquire* (October 1, 1973). https://classic.esquire.com/article/19731001127/print.

Brown, Jared. *Zero Mostel: A Biography*. New York: Atheneum, 1989.

Butterfield, Roger. *LIFE* 14, no. 3 (January 18, 1943).

Encyclopædia Britannica. "Zero Mostel." February 24, 2021. https://www.britannica.com/biography/Zero-Mostel.

Johnston, Laurie. "Theater Hall of Fame Enshrines 51 Artists." *New York Times*, November 19, 1979, sec. C. https://www.nytimes.com/1979/11/19/archives/theater-hall-of-fame-enshrines-51-artists-great-things-and-blank.html.

Kantor, Michael, and Laurence Maslon. "Zero Mostel." Public Broadcasting Service, October 1, 2012. https://www.pbs.org/wnet/broadway/stars/zero-mostel.

McFadden, Robert D. "Zero Mostel Dies of Heart Failure at 62." *New York Times*, September 9, 1977. https://www.nytimes.com/1977/09/09/archives/zero-mostel-dies-of-heart-failure-at-62-zero-mostel-is-dead-at-62.html.

Official Masterworks Broadway. "Zero Mostel." February 25, 2015. https://masterworksbroadway.com/artist/zero-mostel.

Pennsylvania Center for the Book. "Mostel." Pennsylvania State University, 2021. https://pabook.libraries.psu.edu/mostel__zero.

Playbill. "Zero Mostel." 2020. https://www.playbill.com/person/zero-mostel-vault-0000031762.

Simkin, John. Spartacus Educational, January 2020. https://spartacus-educational.com/USAmostel.htm.

Weil, Martin. "Acotr Zero Mostel Dies." *Washington Post*, September 10, 1977. https://www.washingtonpost.com/archive/local/1977/09/10/acotr-zero-mostel-dies/97f111fa-573b-480e-8724-02e056f5cf0a.

Wilner, Norman. "ZERO!" *Esquire* (February 1, 1962). https://classic.esquire.com/article/19620201078/print.

Tony Curtis

Biography. "Tony Curtis." April 12, 2021. https://www.biography.com/actor/tony-curtis.

Davis, Gwen. "Farewell, Tony Curtis." *Vanity Fair*, October 5, 2010. https://www.vanityfair.com/hollywood/2010/10/farewell-tony-curtis.

Encyclopædia Britannica. "Tony Curtis." August 22, 2022. https://www.britannica.com/biography/Tony-Curtis.

Kehr, Dave. "Tony Curtis, Hollywood Leading Man, Dies at 85." *New York Times*, September 30, 2010. https://www.nytimes.com/2010/10/01/movies/01curtis.html.

Ritter, Ken. "Tony Curtis Remembered for Acting Versatility and Artwork." *Christian Science Monitor*, September 30, 2010. https://www.csmonitor.com/The-Culture/Latest-News-Wires/2010/0930/Tony-Curtis-remembered-for-acting-versatility-and-artwork.

Seibold, Witney. "One of Spartacus' Most Important Scenes Was Missing for More than 30 Years." Slash Film, April 13, 2022. https://www.slashfilm.com/831268/one-of-spartacus-most-important-scenes-was-missing-for-more-than-30-years.

Vanguard of Hollywood. "Tony Curtis: The Underrated Actor with Perfect Hair." March 11, 2022. https://vanguardofhollywood.com/star-of-the-month-tony-curtis.

Butterfly McQueen

Alvarez, Lizette. "Butterfly McQueen Dies at 84; Played Scarlett O'Hara's Maid." *New York Times*, December 23, 1995. https://www.nytimes.com/1995/12/23/nyregion/butterfly-mcqueen-dies-at-84-played-scarlett-o-hara-s-maid.html.

JET. "Butterfly McQueen, 84, 'Gone with the Wind' Actress, Dies from Burns." January 15, 1996.

Learmonth, Sarah. "Pioneers of Black Hollywood: Butterfly McQueen—Actor." Heroine Collective, June 7, 2019. http://www.theheroinecollective.com/pioneers-of-black-hollywood-butterfly-mcqueen-actor.

Los Angeles Times. "Actress Butterfly McQueen Is Killed in Fiery Accident." LA Times Archive, December 23, 1995. https://www.latimes.com/archives/la-xpm-1995-12-23-mn-17061-story.html.

Smith, Caroline B.D., and Sara Pendergast. "Butterfly McQueen Biography—Love of Dance Led to Fame, Cast in Gone with the Wind." JRank Articles, 2022. https://biography.jrank.org/pages/2867/Mcqueen-Butterfly.html.

Smith, Justine. "The Bittersweet Legacy of Butterfly McQueen: Actor, Rebel, Trailblazer." Little White Lies, January 7, 2019. https://lwlies.com/articles/butterfly-mcqueen-gone-with-the-wind-black-trailblazer.

Turner Classic Movies. "Butterfly McQueen: What a Character!" YouTube, September 1, 2020. https://www.youtube.com/watch?v=PTDNgs_eUOU.

Vincent, Mal. "Here's to a Beloved Butterfly Who's Gone with the Wind." Virginia Tech Scholarly Communication University Libraries, December 31, 1995. https://scholar.lib.vt.edu/VA-news/VA-Pilot/issues/1995/vp951231/12290089.htm.

Yaeger, Lynn. "Saluting Butterfly McQueen, Who Paved the Way." *Vogue*, January 7, 2017. https://www.vogue.com/article/butterfly-mcqueen-paved-the-way.

YouTube. "Butterfly McQueen." March 4, 2009. https://www.youtube.com/watch?v=Qy90YiCon3M.

Abraham Maslow

Boeree, C. George. "Abraham Maslow." 2006. https://webspace.ship.edu/cgboer/maslow.html.

Chad. "Abraham Maslow Biography—Life of American Psychologist." Totally History, January 4, 2014. https://totallyhistory.com/abraham-maslow.

Cherry, Kendra. "Abraham Maslow Is the Founder of Humanistic Psychology." Verywell Mind, March 16, 2020. https://www.verywellmind.com/biography-of-abraham-maslow-1908-1970-2795524.

Encyclopedia. "Maslow, Abraham." August 25, 2022. https://www.encyclopedia.com/science/dictionaries-thesauruses-pictures-and-press-releases/maslow-abraham.

Encyclopædia Britannica. "Abraham Maslow." June 23, 2022. https://www.britannica.com/biography/Abraham-H-Maslow.

Juma, Norbert. "Abraham Maslow Quotes on Motivation and Being Human." Everyday Power, September 2, 2022. https://everydaypower.com/abraham-maslow-quotes.

New York Times. "Dr. Abraham Maslow, Founder of Humanistic Psychology, Dies." June 10, 1970. https://www.nytimes.com/1970/06/10/archives/dr-abraham-maslow-founder-of-humanistic-psychology-dies.html.

Public Broadcasting Service. "A Science Odyssey: People and Discoveries: Abraham Maslow." 1998. https://www.pbs.org/wgbh/aso/databank/entries/bhmasl.html.

T., Theodore. "Abraham Maslow (Biography + Accomplishments)." Practical Psychology, February 12, 2022. https://practicalpie.com/abraham-maslow.

Zweig, Leonard, and Warren Bennis. "Being Abraham Maslow: Maslow, Abraham H." Internet Archive, Released by Filmmakers Library, January 1, 1972. https://archive.org/details/beingabrahammaslow.

Jonas Salk

American Academy of Achievement. "Jonas Salk, M.D." February 3, 2021. https://achievement.org/achiever/jonas-salk-m-d/#interview.

Forbes. "How Much Money Did Jonas Salk Potentially Forfeit by Not Patenting the Polio Vaccine?" August 9, 2012. https://www.forbes.com/sites/quora/2012/08/09/how-much-money-did-jonas-salk-potentially-forfeit-by-not-patenting-the-polio-vaccine/?sh=259003a569b8.

Jacobs, Charlotte. Jonas Salk: A Life. New York: Oxford University Press, 2018.

Jacobs, Charlotte DeCroes. "Vaccinations Have Always Been Controversial in America: Column." USA Today, August 4, 2015. https://www.usatoday.com/story/opinion/2015/08/04/vaccinations-controversial-america-polio-health/31052179.

Krieger, Jane. "What Price Fame—to Dr. Salk; The Man Who Developed the Polio Vaccine and Became Almost a Folk Hero Overnight Is a Public Figure Against His Will. His One Thought Is to Get Back to His Laboratory." New York Times, July 17, 1955, sec. SM. https://www.nytimes.com/1955/07/17/archives/what-price-fame-to-dr-salk-the-man-who-developed-the-polio-vaccine.html.

National Public Radio. "Among the 1st to Get a Polio Vaccine, Peter Salk Says Don't Rush a COVID-19 Shot." May 30, 2020. https://www.npr.org/transcripts/861887610.

Schmeck, Harold M. "Dr. Jonas Salk, Whose Vaccine Turned Tide on Polio, Dies at 80." *New York Times*, June 24, 1995, sec. 1. https://www.nytimes. com/1995/06/24/obituaries/dr-jonas-salk-whose-vaccine-turned-tide-on-polio-dies-at-80.html.

Robert Aumann

Aumann, Robert. "The Sveriges Riksbank Prize in Economic Sciences in Memory of Alfred Nobel 2005." Nobel Prize Outreach, 2022. https://www.nobelprize. org/prizes/economic-sciences/2005/aumann/biographical.

Biographical Encyclopedia of the Modern Middle East and North Africa. "Aumann, Robert (1930–)." December 29, 2021. https://www.encyclopedia. com/international/encyclopedias-almanacs-transcripts-and-maps/aumann-robert-1930.

Council for the Lindau Nobel Laureate Meetings. "Prof. Dr. Robert J. Aumann." September 11, 2018. https://www.mediatheque.lindau-nobel.org/laureates/aumann.

Davis, M.D., and Steven J. Brams. "Game Theory." Encyclopædia Britannica, December 15, 2021. https://www.britannica.com/science/game-theory.

Encyclopædia Britannica. "Robert J. Aumann." June 4, 2021. https://www.britannica.com/biography/Robert-Aumann.

Hart, Sergiu. "An Interview with Robert Aumann." Einstein Institute of Mathematics, January 2005. http://www.ma.huji.ac.il/hart/papers/md-aumann.pdf.

Madeson, Avital. "Brief Biography." Einstein Institute of Mathematics. http://www.ma.huji.ac.il/raumann/Brief%20Bio.htm.

———. "Robert J Aumann." Einstein Institute of Mathematics. http://www.ma.huji.ac.il/raumann/cv.htm.

UBS. "How Can We End Conflict?" Nobel Perspectives, 2022. https://www.ubs.com/microsites/nobel-perspectives/en/laureates/robert-aumann.html.

Gordon Gekko

CharacTour. "I'm a Match to Gordon Gekko from Wall Street." 2023. https://www.charactour.com/hub/characters/view/Gordon-Gekko.Wall-Street.

Chen, James. "Gordon Gekko: Wall Street's Most Famous Fictional Character?" Investopedia, January 5, 2023. https://www.investopedia.com/terms/g/gordon-gekko.asp.

Clip.Cafe. "'This Is Really a Nice Club, Mr. Gekko. Yeah, Not Bad for a City College Boy. I Bought My…'—Wall Street." December 12, 2020. https://clip.cafe/wall-street-1987/not-bad-a-city-college-boy.

Gornall, Jonathan. "Sleeping Monster Awakes." The National, May 8, 2009. https://www.thenationalnews.com/uae/sleeping-monster-awakes-1.535624.

LinkedIn. "Gordon Gekko—City University of New York City College—New York." 2023. https://www.linkedin.com/in/gordon-gekko-a282b53b.

Movies U-Z, FunTrivia. "Gordon Gekko (Michael Douglas) Is the Villain in the Movie 'Wall Street.'" Which College Did Gekko Attend?" January 10, 2023. https://www.funtrivia.com/en/Movies/Wall-Street-4867.html.

Quotes. "Wall Street." 2022. https://www.quotes.net/movies/wall_street_12385.

Villains Wiki. "Gordon Gekko." 2022. https://villains.fandom.com/wiki/Gordon_Gekko.

Lennie Briscoe

Bernstein, Adam. "'Law & Order' Star Jerry Orbach Dies at 69." *Washington Post*, December 30, 2004. https://www.washingtonpost.com/wp-dyn/articles/A33356-2004Dec29.html.

Brantley, Ben, and Richard Severo. "Jerry Orbach, Star of 'Law & Order,' Dies at 69." *New York Times*, December 29, 2004. https://www.nytimes.com/2004/12/29/arts/jerry-orbach-star-of-law-order-dies-at-69.html?smid=nytcore-ios-share&%3BreferringSource=articleShare.

FanFiction. "Profile of Lennie Briscoe, a Law and Order Fanfic." August 27, 2005. https://www.fanfiction.net/s/2554864/1/Profile-of-Lennie-Briscoe.

Linkedin. "Lennie Briscoe—Detective—27th Precinct." 2023. https://www.linkedin.com/in/lennie-briscoe-640621225.

Toby Ziegler

CharacTour. "I'm a Match to Toby Ziegler from the West Wing." 2023. https://www.charactour.com/hub/characters/view/Toby-Ziegler.The-West-Wing.

Fanlore. "Toby Ziegler." January 20, 2021. https://fanlore.org/wiki/Toby_Ziegler.

Fusion Movies. "All About Celebrity Richard Schiff!" 2022. https://www4.fusionmovies.to/celebrity/kkOuK9FfKO/richard-schiff.

Healy, Patrick D. "A Fictional Presidency Confronts a Leak, Too." *New York Times*, October 29, 2005. https://www.nytimes.com/2005/10/29/arts/television/a-fictional-presidency-confronts-a-leak-too.html?smid=nytcore-ios-share&%3BreferringSource=articleShare.

IMDb. "Richard Schiff." 2023. https://www.imdb.com/name/nm0771493/bio.

Paysden, Michael. "The Infidel." Jewish Telegraph Online, 2010. http://www.jewishtelegraph.com/artinf_6.html.

Politicon. "Richard Schiff." October 18, 2018. https://www.politicon.com/speaker/richard-schiff.

Reid, Joe. "'The Wrath from on High Atop the Thing': The 10 Best Toby Ziegler Episodes of 'The West Wing.'" Decider, May 2, 2017. https://decider.com/2017/05/02/10-best-toby-episodes-of-the-west-wing.

Schiff, Richard. "Richard Schiff's Father Gets Bachelor's Degree." *West Wing News Blog,* January 1, 1970. https://westwingnews.blogspot.com/2006/06/richard-schiffs-father-gets-bachelors.html.

The West Wing Continuity Blog. "Toby Zachary Ziegler." 2022. http://westwing.bewarne.com/toby.html.

West Wing Wiki. "Toby Ziegler." 2022. https://westwing.fandom.com/wiki/Toby_Ziegler.

Don Draper

LinkedIn. "Don Draper—Creative Director—McCann-Erickson Worldwide." 2023. https://www.linkedin.com/in/don-draper-29153aba.

Mad Men Wiki. "Don Draper." 2022. https://madmen.fandom.com/wiki/Don_Draper.

Simpson, Joe. "Mad Men: The Real Don Draper Explained." ScreenRant, July 31, 2020. https://screenrant.com/mad-men-real-don-draper-character-explained.

Sparks, K. "Jon Hamm." Encyclopædia Britannica, August 22, 2022. https://www.britannica.com/biography/Jon-Hamm.

ABOUT
ABRAHAM D. GOLDSMITH

CCNY, BBA, 1934
BROOKLYN LAW SCHOOL
JD, 1938

Abraham D. Goldsmith was a 1934 alumnus of CCNY. His is the story of so many immigrants to America who see City College of New York as their road to realize the American dream.

Goldsmith, the youngest of five children, was born in 1913 in Bessarabia, Romania. When he was one year old, his family fled Europe to escape the pogroms rampant in Romania. They arrived at Ellis Island only to be denied entrance to New York City because the eldest son was diagnosed with TB. Goldsmith's mother, along with her children, returned to Bessarabia, while his father remained in New York City. Three years later, his mother with her children, including then four-year-old Abraham, again came to America, traveling in steerage. This time, the family was allowed entry through the Port of Baltimore and reunited with Goldsmith's father in New York City.

According to the 1915 U.S. Census, Goldsmith's father and his elder brother were fruit peddlers in New York City. His brother would die before the next U.S. Census was completed. The family lived in a tenement in

Harlem. As a boy, Abraham swept hallways in the building to help support his parents and siblings. Much to the pride of his family, he attended CCNY at night, working as a bookkeeper during the day. He then attended Brooklyn Law School at night, working as a CPA during the day, throughout this time supporting his parents and siblings.

Not long after graduation, Goldsmith was drafted into the army and landed in Normandy on D-Day. He became an aide to General Patton and fought for the liberation of Germany and France. As World War II was ending, J. Edgar Hoover posted a job opening for a special agent in Washington, D.C. Applicants had to be CPAs in addition to holding law degrees. Goldsmith was accepted and returned to the United States as a special agent.

Soon after returning to the United States, Goldsmith married and had one daughter, the author of *CCNY Made: Profiles in Grit*, Ronnyjane Goldsmith.

Abraham D. Goldsmith died when he was forty, before he could enjoy the benefits of realizing the American dream.

ABOUT THE AUTHOR

Ronnyjane Goldsmith

Temple University
BA 1968 | MA 1970 | PhD 1981

Through her support of CCNY, Ronnyjane Goldsmith keeps the memory of her father, Abraham D. Goldsmith, alive. While she is not an alumnus, her story is similar to many alumni of CCNY.

Ronnyjane Goldsmith was born in New York City in 1947. Her father, Abraham D. Goldsmith, died when she was seven, and her mother, diagnosed as paranoid schizophrenic, took her own life. Goldsmith describes her parents' influence on her life with a note of irony, writing, "I fortunately inherited my parents' assets and more fortunately overcame their liabilities."

Goldsmith attended eleven public schools in twelve years, including four high schools in three years, graduating with no transcript having a full year of grades and no permanent address. She parlayed a $500 loan into a full scholarship, a Ford Foundation fellowship and a BA, MA and PhD from Temple University. Founded by Russell Conwell in 1884 as a night school, Temple's mission is not dissimilar to the mission on which CCNY was founded.

At a time when options available to women were limited to marriage, teaching or nursing, Goldsmith was one of the first women to be awarded a PhD from Temple University, College of Liberal Arts, but only after the college refused to read her dissertation and denied her the degree for ten years because she was a woman. Although she never uses the title "Dr.," Goldsmith often says the two things of which she is most proud are finally being awarded her PhD and teaching herself how to drive a stick shift, not necessarily in that order.

Goldsmith was inducted into the Temple University Gallery of Success as one of 34 out of 250,000 living alumni who distinguished themselves in their professional careers. In 2011, she was named to the College of Liberal Arts Board of Visitors, a position from which she resigned after two years. These honors did not stop her from speaking out against school policies and appointments she felt were not in the best interest of students, alumni or the university. When Goldsmith was warned of the risks of going against the university administration, she responded with characteristic selfless determination, "What is the worst that can happen?"

In 1972, Goldsmith began her professional career as a public servant, holding appointed positions in Pennsylvania, Maryland and California. As one of the first professional staff hired by the Pennsylvania legislature, she delivered unbiased advice to a politically divided legislature. As fiscal advisor to Baltimore City Council, she ensured that the taxpayers of the city were properly represented despite the intentions of city officials to the contrary. As director of finance for the City of Berkeley, she saved employee pension plans from insolvency and city and pension fund investments from default. And in Los Angeles, as the largest issuer of municipal bonds in the United States, she unraveled bond deals that enriched consultants while costing taxpayers and bond holders millions of dollars. Hired as a "fixer" often as a result of grand jury recommendations, she confronted issues like pay-to-play contracting and corrupt municipal borrowing practices decades before the extent of their cost to the American taxpayer became newsworthy.

The fiscal policies she advanced, well documented by newspapers throughout her career, brought to light conflicts of interest in the public sector that cost taxpayers billions of dollars while enriching the coffers of elected officials, private consultants and labor unions. Goldsmith exposed self-dealing rampant in the public sector by prohibiting the award of management consulting contracts to outside auditors and barring financial advisors from simultaneously serving as municipal bond underwriters. And she attacked the lack of transparency in municipal finance by requiring the disclosure of pension plan liabilities in municipal financial statements making clear to the taxpayer and the bond holder the true cost of labor negotiations and legislative action.

Goldsmith is also known for the retirement and benefit plans she designed, including the Pennsylvania Senior Citizens Property Tax and Rent Assistance Program, which has directed more than $200 billion to programs for elderly citizens since 1972; the Baltimore City Variable Benefit Retirement Plan, which increased benefits for retirees and beneficiaries by up to 17 percent without increasing plan or employee costs; and the City of Berkeley Supplemental Retirement and Income Plan, which preserved and expanded benefits for City of Berkeley employees and Friends of AC Transit that since inception has provided more than two thousand loans to employees facing unforeseen and catastrophic life events.

Most surprising, unlike many of her colleagues, Goldsmith has not benefited from any plan she developed during her years in public service.

While Goldsmith's career as a public servant covered several states and the span of many decades, her successes have two common themes. She prevailed at great risk to herself and her career despite the ceaseless wrath of politicians and consultants who benefited personally and politically from maintaining the status quo. Additionally, millions of people who will never know her name benefit from the programs she designed.

In addition to her public responsibilities, Goldsmith found time to teach at Temple University, Lehigh University and Johns Hopkins University. While still in her twenties, she was a candidate for the state legislature in Pennsylvania. Her slogan as a candidate was "Her place is in the House," reflecting and challenging the norms of the times.

Goldsmith left public service after twenty-five years to become an entrepreneur. When asked why she was leaving public service, Goldsmith explained only partly in jest, "Because all my references are dead, indicted or incarcerated."

As an entrepreneur, Goldsmith has built a private investment management business with clients around the United States. As in the public sector, her solutions for private clients are simple and elegant and many times at odds with prevailing practices. Realizing the inherent conflict between what benefits the advisor and the client, she refuses to recommend proprietary products that benefit the advisor at the expense of the client, complex investments with hidden fees and low returns and annuities that only enrich the advisor when municipal bonds may provide higher income to the client at a much lower cost. Once asked to explain the secret of her success, her answer was again simple and elegant: "No crazy clients. No dead assets.

No proprietary products." Throughout her career in private finance, she has remained critical of an industry where a person's lack of education or experience cannot be held against them when hiring. The outcome, as she describes it, is "an industry dominated by very bad men in very good suits."

In 1998, the same year she became an entrepreneur, Goldsmith secured her place in philanthropy by establishing SIGGiving.* Over the decades, SIGGiving has grown to include programs providing medical assistance to children without hope, programs improving access to higher education for children without family support or financial resources and programs to preserve our national heritage. SIG stands for "Straw into Gold," a moniker used to describe Goldsmith's work in the public sector.

In 2006, Goldsmith established the SIG Fund at the Smile Train. As a result of her donations, more than 300 children received cleft palate operations, giving them new smiles and a second chance at life. In 2012, Goldsmith became a founding donor of Wonderwork. Through her support, each month 3 children received life-changing medical assistance. As a result, by December 2017 more than 175 children had received the gift of sight. In 2020, Goldsmith became a Ronald McDonald House sponsor. Ronald McDonald House provides room and board for families so they may remain close to their children hospitalized due to catastrophic illness.

In 2007, Goldsmith endowed the SIG Scholarship at Temple University. She endowed this scholarship so that the dreams and professional aspirations of students who lost their parents might come true. If it weren't for the financial assistance Temple University provided to her, Goldsmith could not have attended college. Nor would she have been able to take advantage of the professional opportunities she could only dream about as a seventeen-year-old without financial resources or family support. In 2011, Goldsmith established the 57 Cent Fund at Temple University. The fund is named in memory of Hattie May Wiatt, who died in 1886 at five years of age and left Dr. Russell Conwell fifty-seven cents, the seed money used to establish Temple University. In 2021, when Goldsmith was seventy-five, her first book, *Temple Made: Profiles in Grit*, was published. Proceeds from the sale of *Temple Made* were dedicated to the Alumni Scholarship Fund at Temple University.

In memory of her father, in 2010 Goldsmith endowed the Abraham D. Goldsmith SIG Scholarship at CCNY. The scholarship is awarded to outstanding students whose parents came to America seeking a better life

---

* It was not until almost twenty years after she received her PhD that Goldsmith realized that rather than being resentful because of the lack of choices she had in her youth, she should be grateful for the opportunities afforded her—opportunities she meticulously chronicled every year in the most unlikely of places: her obituary.

for their children. In 2018, Goldsmith established the Delancey Street Fund at CCNY. The fund is named after the street of the same name in New York City that gave immigrants to America a chance for a better life. The Delancey Street Fund, like the 57 Cent Fund, provides assistance to students without financial resources who are facing catastrophic life events. In 2023, Goldsmith's second book, *CCNY Made: Profiles in Grit*, was published. Proceeds from the sale of the book are dedicated to the Delancey Street Fund.

As of 2022, forty-two SIG Scholarships have been awarded.

Goldsmith has received the highest honor from CCNY, being named to the President's Circle, an award that recognizes visionary supporters who have made City College a priority in their philanthropy.

Goldsmith's affiliation with the National Portrait Gallery in Washington, D.C., began in 2012, when she adopted the portrait of Lucretia Mott on display at the gallery. Lucretia Mott—abolitionist, suffragette and founder of Swarthmore College—established the village of La Mott in Montgomery County, Pennsylvania, where Mott donated the land and built homes for slaves escaping from the South through the Underground Railroad. La Mott is located in the former 154th Legislative District, where in her youth Goldsmith was a candidate for the state legislature.

In 2014, Goldsmith adopted the Rembrandt Peale portrait of George Washington, the first president of the United States, patriot and philanthropist.

In 2016, Goldsmith adopted the portrait of Alexander Hamilton, author of the Federalist Papers and the first secretary of the U.S. Treasury. Hamilton's portrait is on the front of the ten-dollar bill.

In 2021, Goldsmith adopted the portraits of Susan B. Anthony and Elizabeth Cady Stanton. In 1848, Anthony, along with Elizabeth Cady Stanton and Lucretia Mott, officially launched the women's rights movement in the United States. In 2016, it was announced that Lucretia Mott, Susan B. Anthony and Elizabeth Cady Stanton are three of the five women whose faces will grace the back of the ten-dollar bill. A monument of the three women is on permanent display in the Capitol Rotunda.

Goldsmith has sponsored several exhibits at the National Portrait Gallery, including *The Art of Elaine de Kooning* (2015); *The Face of Battle* (2017); *The Sweat of Their Face* (2017); *The American Presidents Gallery* (2018); *Votes for Women* (2019); and *Every Eye Is Upon Me: First Ladies of the United States* (2020). In 2018, Goldsmith provided support for the acquisition of the earliest known photograph of a U.S. president, John Quincy Adams, for the permanent collection of the National Portrait Gallery. In 2017,

Goldsmith was named to the Host Committee of the Smithsonian representing the National Portrait Gallery.

In 2022, Goldsmith donated her collection of Arion Press books to the Smithsonian Library. The collection of 103 Arion titles became part of the Smithsonian's American Art and Portrait Gallery Library. With the gift, the Smithsonian Libraries and Archives has one of the most complete public collections of Arion Press's work in Washington, D.C.

Goldsmith's dedication to Temple University and CCNY continues today as she works to establish a program where every year alumni from each school will purchase one copy of either *Temple Made: Profiles in Grit* or *CCNY Made: Profiles in Grit* and give the book to a freshman. In Goldsmith's own words, this is a win-win-win. First, by purchasing a copy of the book at a small cost, an otherwise uninvolved alumni will become involved with their alma mater. Second, by giving a copy of the book to a freshman, the freshman will learn about the footsteps they are following. And third, the proceeds from book sales are dedicated to scholarships and emergency grants for students who might not otherwise be able to attend or graduate college.

Goldsmith currently divides her time between Palm Beach, Washington, D.C., and San Francisco. She does not plan on retiring, still determined to make her obituary Sunday *New York Times*–worthy.